The Church and AI

Seven Guidelines for Ministry
on the Digital Frontiers

David Betts

ALL RIGHTS RESERVED

No part of this publication may be reproduced, stored in a retrieval system, or transmitted, in any form or by any means—electronic, mechanical, photocopying, recording, or otherwise--without prior written permission.

All Scripture quotations have been taken from the Christian Standard Bible®, Copyright © 2017 by Holman Bible Publishers. Used by permission. Christian Standard Bible® and CSB® are federally registered trademarks of Holman Bible Publishers.

Copyright © 2024 by David Betts

ISBN: 978-1-0688065-0-6

John 3:30

He must increase, but I must decrease.

Acknowledgments

To Jorin Green, an ever-present supporter in my academic studies and an early sounding board for the ideas that formed this book. To Dustin Burlet, few have championed this book as much as you have, for which I am incredibly grateful. Thanks to Denae Lappin, Ryan Peters, Donelle Hadley, Melanie Dzugan, and Jack Coupland, who all gave their time to support the editing process.

Serving as the lead elder at Trinity Church, Red Deer, is one of my greatest joys. Your unwavering support and encouragement—along with that of our dear friends at Ascot Life Church—has meant the world.

I want to give special thanks to my wife, Sharaya. You have willingly sacrificed so much to allow me to write this book. Though you may not get the public credit you deserve for this team effort, I am eternally grateful for who you are and the privilege of sharing this life together. I love you.

Finally, all praise be to God, the author of creation, the hero of my story, and the subject of this book. May this small offering glorify you in some way.

CONTENTS

Introduction	1
Part One: The Current AI Landscape	**7**
A Short History of AI	9
Understanding the Current AI Landscape	30
Part Two: **Seven Guidelines for Navigating** **the Digital Frontiers**	**46**
Introduction to the Seven Guidelines	48
Guideline One: Prioritize Relationships	55
Guideline Two: Nurture Resilient Congregations	91
Guideline Three: Build Adaptability into Church Structures	114
Guideline Four: Embrace Positive Technological Developments	139
Guideline Five: Stay Informed in a Rapidly Changing Environment	163
Guideline Six: Be Proactive in Praying for God-given Wisdom	193
Guideline Seven: Keep an Undistracted Focus on the Church's Mission	217
Conclusion	241
Bibliography	249

Introduction

Artificial intelligence will transform our lives. For many of us—whether we realize it or not—it already has. AI is undoubtedly a technological marvel, but it provides believers with unprecedented challenges in unprecedented times. In an article for *The Atlantic* in 2023, Jacob Stern explains why AI is so unique:

> AI is not really a single issue you can be for or against the way you can with, say, guns or abortion. It is, to name just a few aspects, an economic issue (Will it replace millions of jobs?), a foreign-policy issue (What if China surpasses [the USA]?), and a political issue (Is it about to supercharge our misinformation problem?). But there is one overarching debate about AI: between the techno-utopians who think it will usher in a

new age of prosperity and the techno-pessimists who think it will be a destructive, destabilizing force that might just usher in the end of the world.[1]

I'm not sure a dichotomy is helpful here. It's not either/or. It's both/and. You've likely heard about the suddenly ubiquitous ChatGPT, an AI-driven chatbot that exploded onto the scene in late 2022 and early 2023 faster than any other social media platform or app ever had. We're probably all familiar with Siri, Alexa, and the possibility of self-driving cars. It's difficult to avoid the countless conversations about AI in the news. But here's the problem: as the global Church, I'm concerned we're missing the forest for the trees. I fear that generally speaking, we're collectively choosing to see AI as a novelty and not an agent for utterly changing how we live, work, and minister in the world. There are important questions to answer that go far beyond "Can ChatGPT write my sermon illustration for me?"

Consider some of the following issues:

- How does AI affect church leadership?
- What does AI mean for pastoral care?
- What are AI's theological implications?
- What are the future economic and societal effects of AI? What does this mean for ministry?
- What are the strengths, weaknesses, opportunities, and threats of AI for the Church at large?
- How does the Church respond to existential questions around superintelligence and transhumanism?

Introduction

These critical questions warrant thoughtful reflection, but there is so little out there for the believing community right now. I wrote this book to provide an early offering that, Lord willing, may help followers of Jesus—whether church leaders, ministry leaders, or laypeople—wrestle with the growing proliferation of artificial intelligence in our world.

When I was around five, my parents gave my twin brother and me an old second-hand computer. The pre-Internet age neutered any potential dangers of this early PC—in fact, a modem wouldn't find its way into our house for several more years—and it was simple and empty enough in those days that, were we to corrupt it in some way (which was highly likely), a mere floppy disk could wipe the computer and reinstall the relatively primitive operating system. It was an enormous privilege at such a young age; we had the freedom to pretend we knew how computers worked, click buttons we didn't understand, and experiment, knowing there weren't any consequences if we did something wrong. Honestly, we mostly drew pictures of starry night skies on Microsoft Paint. Since then, I've always had a keen interest in technology, so when conversations about AI exploded into the mainstream, I wondered—like many others—how these developments might impact the Church.

I'm perhaps more technically minded than the average person, but I'm no programmer. I'm a pastor with *just enough* technical knowledge to follow developments with interest and to understand conversations with my computer science genius friend David Hulme (no, not the Scottish philosopher David Hume). I'm also passionate enough about the body of Christ to wonder what the future holds for it in light of AI developments.

A while ago, I was privileged to have the unique opportunity to dedicate a large chunk of my Master of Divinity studies to AI's possible impact on the Church, which even further piqued my growing passion for the subject. A long-form academic paper became a series of blog posts; that blog became this book. At the center of each of these mediums was a core belief that we—the Church—are in dire need of deep discussion about what artificial intelligence will do to our society, coupled with a growing conviction that there are seven essential guidelines that the Church must follow to navigate an increasingly AI-driven world successfully:

Seven Guidelines for Ministry on the Digital Frontiers

1. Prioritize Relationships.
2. Nurture Resilient Congregations.
3. Build Adaptability into Church Structures.
4. Embrace Positive Technological Developments.
5. Stay Informed in a Rapidly Changing Environment.
6. Be Proactive in Praying for God-Given Wisdom.
7. Keep an Undistracted Focus on the Mission of the Church.

Are these the only guidelines? Almost certainly not. But in the ever-changing world of artificial intelligence, they provide a solid, gospel-focused foundation for seeking and serving God while the sands of change shift around us. Because the landscape of AI is developing so quickly, it seems that it's a fool's errand to focus primarily on specific use cases for AI. If you're looking for a guide to *implementing* AI in your churches, you'll likely finish the book disappointed. We'll allow ourselves the opportunity to engage our imaginations occasionally, but our focus will be narrowed to the broader impacts and possibly even existential issues that AI may bring about.

In terms of methodology, the approach is reasonably straightforward: Part One is short, focusing on helping believers get up to speed together. Chapter One explores a brief history of AI and expressly intends to highlight that artificial intelligence isn't simply a fad. In actual fact, it's been hovering around the computer science consciousness for almost a Century and warrants much deeper thought than many of us have—up to this point—been willing to give. Chapter Two then explores the current AI landscape, defining several key terms and concepts that will benefit the rest of our journey.

Part Two explores the seven guidelines in detail. Rather than barraging you with the potential impact of AI from the outset, this book will take a gentler approach. Each chapter will add slightly more detail to our growing understanding of AI so that we have a reasonably broad understanding of the topic as a whole by the end of the guidelines.

I pray that the following pages will bless you as you seek to engage with a world increasingly entwined with artificial intelligence. The challenges we face as the Church are notable but not insurmountable. After all, as the apostle Paul writes in Romans 8:31, if God is for us, who can be against us?

NOTES

[1] Jacob Stern, "Where's the AI Culture War?," *The Atlantic*, last modified April 9, 2023, accessed May 19, 2023, https://www.theatlantic.com/technology/archive/2023/04/generative-ai-tech-elon-musk-chatgpt-politics-biden/673673/.

PART ONE:

The Current AI Landscape

A Short History of AI

All of us will approach artificial intelligence with some degree of bias. Perhaps we conjure up images of nefarious He-Who-Must-Not-Be-Named-Like supervillains set on world domination and mass destruction. Maybe we see AI as the digital white knight in shining armor, here to usher in an almost-but-not-quite heavenly utopia.

The irony with AI is that while endless streams of ones and zeroes brought AI into existence, a binary approach to understanding it will do us little good.

As with most well-written characters, artificial intelligence is far from two-dimensional. It transcends the boundaries of good and evil and black and white. It manifests a multidimensional and textured reality that defies simple classification as much as we might long for one. Artificial intelligence and its future is complex, nuanced, and enigmatic, dependent on innumerable factors and considerations. Just as the backstory is vital to any character with depth, we can learn an awful lot from AI's meandering journey to its current form.

For that reason, to understand today's artificial intelligence—which will most likely be outdated when you read these words—it's helpful to dig into AI's history. You might be disappointed if you're looking for a comprehensive, play-by-play analysis of this technology's rise. This chapter aims to arrive at a relatively broad understanding of key moments that will help us contextualize some of the enormous changes that have taken place in the last decade and move towards a healthy, considered response as the body of Christ.

Strangely, our journey towards understanding AI starts not in the laboratories of tech giants like Google and Meta but in the mists of time, with a 2700-year-old Mediterranean myth. As we uncover the layers of AI's history, we'll discover how humanity's obsession with intelligent machines has led us to this challenging juncture on the world's timeline.

Dreams of the First Robots

We begin south of the Greek mainland, on the largest of the 6,000 islands and islets from which the nation is comprised. This island is Crete, bordered by crisp white beaches and a sea that gleams the sort of shimmering turquoise that makes you wonder if the seabed is covered with those rare, precious stones that bear the same name. It's many centuries before the birth of Christ, and as the sun sets, the aroma of freshly caught fish sizzling on the fire wafts enticingly across the dry, sun-scorched hills. A dull rhythmic thump echoes in the distance, subsides, and returns a few seconds later, too repetitive to be thunder but too loud to be anything of human origin. To the people of Crete, it's just a part of life, but to those would-be invaders looking to attack from the horizons of the Mediterranean Sea, those distant rumbles bring unimaginable terror with them.

They are the hulking footsteps of Talos.

According to Greek mythology, Talos was a bronze automaton fashioned by Hephaestus, fused with a magical substance called ichor and made in man's image. It was roughly the size of New York's iconic Statue of Liberty and had the sole objective of protecting the island from encroaching raiders. The Cretian locals tell stories of how this monstrous giant lurched with considerable menace around Crete's picturesque 1,046km (650 miles) perimeter, ready at a moment's notice to hurl chariot-sized boulders at any ships who dared come within his mighty range.

Of course, we know that Talos was nothing more than a myth, but there's more to this story than meets the eye. According to Stanford scholar Adrienne Mayor in her book *Gods and Robots*, this is just one of *many* stories about "animated statues and self-moving devices" found in Greek antiquity.[1] She suggests that in Talos, humanity may have found one of the earliest conceptions of artificial intelligence. Little more than a spark—a whiff, a dream—but there nevertheless. Mayer explains:

> The exact definition of the term robot is debatable, but the basic conditions are met by Talos: a self-moving android with a power source that provides energy, 'programmed' to 'sense' its surroundings and possessing a kind of 'intelligence' or way of processing data to 'decide' to interact with the environment to perform actions or tasks.[2]

Or what about Pandora? She's an echo of Eve, who we know as the first woman created by a loving and good God (Gen. 2:23-24). The difference is that Pandora is another being in ancient Greek mythology and the creation of Hephaestus (who seems to be fairly adept at creating not-quite-humans), shaped from clay, and gifted with a forbidden and not-to-be-opened box that contained all the world's evil. Perhaps, Mayor suggests, this Pandora of Greek mythology was also an early conception of artificial intelligence. She believes that Hesiod's original description of Pandora reveals "an artificial, evil woman built by Hephaestus and sent to Earth on the orders of Zeus to punish humans for discovering fire" and whose primary objective was to "infiltrate the human world and release her jar of miseries."[3]

As Mayor readily admits, it's difficult to know how these ancient people viewed self-moving, seemingly self-thinking entities in the murky mythological world of the Greeks. Was Talos the world's first visualization of a robot? Was he sentient? Did he have a soul? Was he viewed as a technological machination or a marvel of magic?

We don't know.

But what we *do* know is this: when Jesus began his ministry, stories of "android[s] with encoded instructions to carry out complex activities" would have been familiar in the society in which he and his disciples lived.[4] In other words, Jesus would probably have known the tales of Talos and Pandora in his Hellenized setting. Perhaps he would have even been familiar with the Jewish Golem, the convoluted and ever-evolving tale of primitive, mystical artificial intelligence which found its roots in the Hebrew word *galmi* in Psalm 139:16 but of which little else was written before the compilation of the Babylonian Talmud a few centuries after the Jesus' resurrection.[5]

In light of these myths, it's worth noting that Jesus could have utilized fledgling Jewish or long-held Gentile mythology as a jumping-off point to prime his followers for the potentially existential realities of AI that lurked in a distant millennium. He could easily have said, "Dear friends, do you remember Talos and Pandora from Greek mythology? One day, something like this will be a reality. . . here's what you should do."

But he didn't.

Here's why this matters: some semblance of artificial intelligence *as an idea* has hovered around the shores of Crete and in the human imagination for *centuries*. However, the quest to achieve artificial intelligence wouldn't begin until the 1930s, when a young British mathematician named Alan Turing would enter the picture.

Alan Turing

Turing was born in Maida Vale, England, on June 23, 1912, and his life was defined by exceptional ability. He was not quite ten when his teachers began to recognize the prodigious talent of the child, describing him as something of a genius.[6] This early recognition of his considerable abilities would set the stage for a short-lived but remarkable career in the world of computer science.

At King's College, Cambridge, Turing flourished. Indeed, his intellectual gifting was such that, after a lunch meeting with John Maynard Keynes, the prominent economist wrote to his wife, "I had to lunch today the Fellowship candidate who seems much the cleverest on paper . . . He is <u>excellent</u> – there cannot be a shadow of doubt . . .Turing is his name."[7]

In 1936, at just twenty-four years old, he authored a groundbreaking paper titled *On Computable Numbers, with an Application to the Entscheidungsproblem*. Despite its somewhat unremarkable title, this paper revolutionized the computing world by introducing the concept of universality concerning computation.[8] Universality refers to the idea that a single machine could be designed to perform a multitude of tasks, such as arithmetic, machine translation, chess, speech understanding, and animation. In other words, to quote prominent present-day computer scientist Stuart Russell, "One machine [could do] it all."[9] Before Turing's work, computers were often designed for specific tasks, and creating a new machine for each problem was cumbersome and impractical. Turing's notion of universality laid the foundations for developing general-purpose computers that could be programmed to handle a range of diverse tasks with powerful efficiency.

The essence of Turing's insight lay in his proposal of what would eventually come to be known as a "universal Turing machine." He demonstrated that this hypothetical machine could execute any computational task that could be described in terms of algorithms. In other words, Turing recognized that, in principle, intelligence could be artificially simulated. Such an idea was groundbreaking, changing how people thought about computation and eventually paving the way for the personal computers and programming languages that define the digital age we live in today. We can only imagine what Turing would have thought of the tiny supercomputers we call "smartphones" that accompany many of us wherever we go today.

The contributions of this young mathematician's gifted mind did not end here. After almost two years of walking the Collegiate-Gothic architecture of Princeton University, Turing lent his gifts to a team of cryptanalysts at Bletchley Park, where he focused on cracking German codes during the Second World War. His work at Bletchley Park, along with the efforts of other talented codebreakers, had a significant impact on the outcome of the war and would eventually be depicted in the award-winning 2014 film *The Imitation Game*, which starred Benedict Cumberbatch and Keira Knightly and introduced his achievements to a more mainstream audience.

After the war, Turing continued his exploration of artificial intelligence. Fourteen years after publishing *On Computable Numbers, with an Application to the Entscheidungsproblem* and fresh from his incredible feats of codebreaking genius, Turing published another seminal paper: *On Computing Machinery and Intelligence*. In this work, he conceptualized the imitation game and what would eventually become known as the "Turing Test," an evaluation of a machine's capacity to demonstrate intelligent behavior at a level comparable to—or indiscernible from—an average human being.[10]

The Turing Test created a critical juncture in AI's story because—in theory, at least—it provided a practical, objective method for measuring the intelligence of machines. Turing's proposal captured the imagination of the public and ignited enthusiasm for the possibility of creating machines that could mimic human intelligence. Suddenly, the tales of Talos, Golem, and even Dorothy's Tin Man (who had relatively recently graced the silver screen in 1939's *The Wizard of* Oz) were no longer pure science fiction; there was a sense of tangible propulsion toward the ultimate goal of putting artificial intelligence within reach of scientific reality.

Turing's visionary ideas and groundbreaking research laid the groundwork for the digital age and the ongoing pursuit of artificial intelligence. His legacy continues to inspire researchers and engineers in their quest to create ever-more sophisticated machines capable of learning, reasoning, and interacting with the world in ways that were once deemed solely human attributes. Today, Turing is rightly celebrated as one of the pioneers of modern computing and artificial intelligence, and his contributions to the field have shaped the way we live, work, and interact with technology.

The 1950s and 1960s

Despite Alan Turing's obvious intellectual prowess and monumental contributions to computer science, his life was marked by inner struggles, and he tragically took his own life shortly before his 42nd birthday, only a few years after publishing *On Computing Machinery and Intelligence*. Nonetheless, his work and ideas sparked something of a surge of activity in the field of artificial intelligence during the remainder of the 1950s.

Turing's work was followed in 1956 by the Dartmouth Summer Research Project, a pivotal moment in the history of artificial intelligence. In the hallowed halls of this esteemed Ivy League New Hampshire College, John McCarthy, the Assistant Professor of Mathematics, along with Marvin Minsky, Nathaniel Rochester and Claude Shannon, submitted a proposal for a project which sought to discover "how to make machines use language, form abstractions and concepts, solve [the] kinds of problems now reserved for humans, and improve themselves."[11] Building upon Turing's ideas, the Dartmouth Summer Research Project acted as a catalyst, propelling artificial intelligence into the forefront of scientific exploration and the beginning of a new digital frontier. Indeed, it was during this project that the term "artificial intelligence" was first coined.

In 1957, just one year after the project at Dartmouth College, Sir Julian Huxley published an essay introducing *transhumanism* as a concept for the first time. Transhumanism emerged as a significant idea that demanded the attention of society and will increasingly require the attention of the Church. It's a concept we'll explore later in this book, but at its core, transhumanism seeks to leverage scientific and technological advancements to augment human capabilities and, in its most radical form, transcend the human body's limitations by uploading consciousness into a digital medium. Huxley believed "the human species [would] be on the threshold of a new kind of existence . . . consciously fulfilling its real destiny."[12]

Interestingly, transhumanism wasn't entirely new. Julian Huxley's brother, Aldous, had explored similar things in his 1932 dystopian classic, *Brave New World*, offering early glimpses into a future where science and technology could profoundly influence human development.

As the 1960s unfolded, the scientific and philosophical communities began grappling with the notion of *superintelligence*. Among those engaged in this discussion was Irving John Good, a British mathematician, scientist, and former colleague of Alan Turing at Bletchley Park. In 1966, Good introduced the time *ultraintelligence* to the world—a precursor to the concept of superintelligence—and delved into the profound implications of machines potentially surpassing human cognitive abilities.

Good's influential paper, *Speculations Concerning the First Ultraintelligent Machines*, predicted that the rise of ultraintelligence would "unquestionably" lead to an "intelligence explosion, [where] the intelligence of man would be left far behind."[13] This notion raised important questions about the potential consequences and ethical considerations surrounding the development and control of artificial superintelligence.

The 1950s and 1960s marked a pivotal period in the development of artificial intelligence, shaping the very foundations of the field as we know it today. In the fast-paced and sensationalized landscape of the 21st Century, it is all too easy to succumb to doom-mongering, exaggerated claims, and conspiracy theories driven by the relentless algorithms of social media and the never-ending pursuit of ad revenue over objectivity. As we delve deeper into the potential future of AI, you may encounter concepts and predictions that seem far-fetched, tempting you to dismiss the potential of this technology as nothing more than a ridiculous fantasy. I can certainly understand such skepticism; indeed, there is something refreshingly human about it. However, dear reader, please do not miss that some of the finest minds of past generations foresaw the potential issues associated with artificial intelligence long before it was anything more than a figment of the imagination and all during a time when sensationalist media held considerably less sway over intellectual discourse.

When we explore the realms of artificial general intelligence (AGI), superintelligence, and transhumanism, we're not simply chasing after the latest passing trend. Rather, we're grappling with issues at the forefront of intellectual discourse for many decades and multiple generations.

These are anything but fads; they're enduring considerations that have challenged humanity for a considerable time. The difference is that what was once consigned to the realm of imagination is on the precipice of our reality.

But let's get back to history.

The AI Winters

Conceptual developments and ideas around artificial intelligence advanced somewhat quickly during the 1950s and 1960s. However, progression slowed drastically in the 1970s, an era that witnessed the onset of what is now commonly called the "first AI winter." During this period, the field faced significant challenges that hindered its progress, including technological limitations and a lack of funding, leading to a general sense of inactivity and stagnation until around 1980.[14]

Pioneers of AI research had worked tirelessly to explore various approaches to developing systems that could match—and possibly surpass—human capabilities. However, researchers made many bold but unfulfilled predictions in their zeal for success, and their support suffered for it. While these early attempts at creating AI systems showed potential, they were far from achieving what they had set out to accomplish. Primitive artificial intelligence couldn't cope with ambiguity or uncertainty, producing underwhelming results and making them unsuitable for handling real-world problems effectively. As it turns out, unintelligent artificial intelligence is a tough sell.

Furthermore, the computational power available at the time was limited, severely hampering the development of sophisticated AI algorithms. Governments and corporations became skeptical about supporting a field that seemed to offer little practical progress, and funding dried up. Evidently, the world was not quite ready for artificial intelligence, and the first AI winter set in.

For almost a decade, cold disinterest gripped the field like the frigid and vicious bite of a Canadian deep freeze on the

Prairies. However, after what must have seemed like an age to those passionate about artificial intelligence, the early 1980s brought about crucial developments that rekindled interest in AI and set the stage for its eventual resurgence. One of the most significant factors that thawed cooling interest in the field was the rise of personal computers (PCs). In one of the most important events in computer history, IBM released the personal computer in 1981. Two years later, Apple introduced the first mass-marketed computer with a graphical user interface (or GUI). While the latter was prohibitively expensive for most consumers, it changed the computing landscape and opened the way for much cheaper alternatives. At the time of writing, Apple's latest project, the *Apple Vision Pro*, may do the same. Time will tell.

The advent of affordable and accessible computers empowered a broader audience to experiment with programming and technology. This democratization of computing power and the release of simpler programming languages like C++ in 1985 allowed researchers and enthusiasts to explore AI algorithms and build rudimentary AI applications on a smaller scale. Such changes brought computer programming into the mainstream, sparking interest in software development and technical skills among the general public. This newfound technological enthusiasm paved the way for new generations of AI researchers who would later contribute to the field's revitalization.

Japan's bold investment in the Fifth-Generation Computer Systems Project was another critical factor that would prove pivotal in reviving interest in AI. Launched in the early 1980s, this ambitious endeavor aimed to surpass Western efforts in achieving artificial intelligence. Relations between Japan and the US were tense and uneasy in light of changing international dynamics, accusations of espionage and unfair trade practices concerning technology. During this time, the Japanese government looked to take what they viewed as a "positive step in the creation of a new international relationship for Japan with the West, indeed with the whole world."[15] As such, they allocated a staggering $400 million over a decade to develop supercomputers capable of advanced computations, natural language processing, and solving complex problems. In other words, they sought to become world leaders in artificial intelligence.

The Fifth-Generation Computer Systems Project captured the attention of the international AI community and injected a renewed sense of competition and excitement into the field. Japan poured unprecedented resources into AI research, forcing other countries to try to keep up, igniting a race to push the boundaries of the technology.

Unfortunately, despite encouraging developments that showed some promise, AI research faced significant challenges. The complexity of replicating human intelligence in machines, limited computational power, and inadequate algorithms hindered any significant progress in achieving genuine artificial intelligence. While there was some success with narrow AI systems which could excel at specific tasks, the ultimate goal of creating machines with human-like intelligence remained elusive. Nevertheless, although the Fifth-Generation Computer Systems Project did not achieve what it intended, it catapulted AI back into the forefront of discussions.

Following the failure of Japan's ambitious project, artificial intelligence again found itself in a period of decline in the early 1990s, which has since become known as the "second AI winter." Like the first AI winter, technological limitations and failures became more apparent and as a result, enthusiasm and funding declined. The public and corporate interest in AI dwindled, and the once-promising technology seemed to be losing its allure.

Despite the obvious challenges of the second AI winter, small pockets of progress and a few notable achievements kept AI's flame burning. One of the most significant victories during this period was IBM's "Deep Blue" project. Deep Blue was a supercomputer designed specifically to play chess at a grandmaster level. It culminated years of research in parallel computing, machine learning, and chess-specific heuristics. In the first of several historic moments for AI, Deep Blue faced off against the reigning world chess champion, Garry Kasparov. The year was 1996, and in a stunning upset, Deep Blue defeated Kasparov in the opening game, becoming the first computer program to win against a reigning world chess champion in a classical format. While Kasparov eventually won the match, Deep Blue's victory marked a pivotal moment for AI and demonstrated that machines could compete at the highest levels of human intellectual endeavors.

The following year, on May 11, 1997, Kasparov again faced IBM's supercomputer for a six-game match. Photographers and camera crews gathered on the 35th floor of Manhattan's Equitable Center, and palpable anticipation filled the room as the chess grandmaster sat down to face his greatest digital opponent in another thrilling encounter.

Kasparov won the first game.
Deep Blue took the second.

Game three: draw.
Game four: draw.
Game five: draw.

It was a tighter contest than any had expected. Kasparov went into the final game with the match on the line. IBM's Deep Blue sacrificed its knight, obliterating Kasparov's defense. Deep Blue's human counterpart rested his head in his hands before doing something his artificial nemesis couldn't: he stood up and walked away from the table, hands raised in exasperation. Deep Blue had won.

In a historic turn of events, one of the greatest chess champions in history had lost a full match to a computer. Deep Blue's success garnered significant attention and ignited debates about the capabilities and limitations of AI. Some saw it as groundbreaking, while others argued that the victory merely demonstrated brute computational force and lacked true understanding or intelligence.

AI's Big Bang

Despite the triumphs of Deep Blue and other notable achievements during the second AI winter, the field continued to face significant challenges. The technology was still not yet mature enough to fulfil the grand vision of creating intelligent machines that could understand and reason like humans across various tasks. AI researchers continued to grapple with the limitations of existing algorithms and the need for more sophisticated approaches to address complex real-world problems. But everything would change a decade into the 21st Century.

A Short History of AI

In a dramatic turning point in AI's history, the field experienced what many now refer to as "AI's Big Bang," driving a revolutionary breakthrough in neural networks and deep learning. At the forefront of this transformation was the pioneering work of Geoff Hinton, a renowned researcher in the field of machine learning and artificial neural networks, terms that we'll explore in the next chapter. In 2012, Hinton and his colleagues achieved a significant milestone in AI research when they won the ImageNet competition, a critical challenge in computer vision. They utilized deep learning techniques—particularly a type of artificial neural network called a *convolutional* neural network (CNNs)—to dramatically improve the ability of a computer to recognize images artificially. Once again, these are terms that we'll discuss soon, so don't panic if you've never heard them before. For now, it's enough to understand that a CNN is designed to process and understand visual information in much the same way the brain processes visual information by detecting edges, shapes, and objects. It's how the native photos app on most smartphones can distinguish cats from cookies and mountains from monkeys. This breakthrough propelled computer vision to new heights and transformed the way AI researchers approached various tasks.

Deep learning is a complicated concept, but what matters for our purposes is that its success in supporting computer vision sparked an explosion of interest and investment in AI research. Corporations and governments worldwide suddenly recognized the transformative potential of AI in various industries, from social media to self-driving cars, which meant the race was on to become industry leaders. Major technology companies such as Google, Meta, Microsoft, and Amazon started investing heavily in AI research and development, creating dedicated research labs and acquiring AI startups to stay at the forefront of the competition. As companies jostled for power, so did nations. At the time of writing, the USA and China lead the way in an arm wrestle for AI superiority.

But all of this has happened in an extremely short period of time. As a result, the rapid progress of AI technologies has also led to renewed discussions about its ethical implications. The growing deployment of autonomous systems and AI-powered algorithms has raised questions about privacy, bias, accountability, and potential economic and cultural impacts—much of the focus of this book. Governments and regulatory bodies began grappling with the challenges of creating frameworks to govern AI technologies responsibly and ensure that AI is used for the betterment of society.

On November 30, 2022, Open AI released an early version of "ChatGPT," an AI-powered conversational agent known as a large language model (LLM) designed to engage with users through something called "natural language processing." It's a simple idea: users give the system a "prompt," and LLM gives an intelligent response. The release of ChatGPT quickly became a viral sensation, capturing the general public's imagination and sparking widespread interest in AI. In the last few years, businesses have scrambled to incorporate customized versions of ChatGPT or its growing alternatives into their systems.

The ability of LLMs like ChatGPT to generate coherent and contextually relevant responses showcases the progress made in natural language understanding and human-machine interaction. People from all walks of life started using ChatGPT for various processes, from entertainment and companionship to educational assistance and professional support. More recently, OpenAI released Sora, which turns a prompt into a fully functional video of staggering realism. Google has released technology that creates music from similar prompts. Meta has released translational tools. The list goes on. Organizations are incorporating AI into their workflows in ways that are beginning to alter the fabric of our society at a fundamental level.

Humanity has never been closer to realizing those ancient Greek dreams of Talos. What happens next will inevitably transform the world as we know it, but precisely how that looks remains to be seen.

We're standing at the fringes of the digital frontiers. Enormous change is coming, whether we like it or not.

NOTES

¹ Adrienne Mayor, *Gods and Robots* (Princeton, NJ: Princeton University Press, 2018), 37.

² Ibid., 41.

³ Stanford University, "Ancient Myths Reveal Early Fantasies about Artificial Life," *Stanford News*, February 28, 2019, accessed May 22, 2023, https://news.stanford.edu/2019/02/28/ancient-myths-reveal-early-fantasies-artificial-life/.

⁴ Ibid., 42.

⁵ In Sanhedrin 65b of the Talmud, Rava creates a Golem, but because it cannot speak, Rabbi Zeira refuses to recognize it as human. It is generally accepted that Sanhedrin 65 was written between the 3rd and 6th Centuries.

⁶ Nigel Cawthorne, *Alan Turing: The Enigma Man*, E Book. (Arcturus Publishings Limited, 2014), 15.

⁷ "Alan Mathison Turing (1912-54)," *King's College Cambridge*, accessed August 7, 2023, https://www.kings.cam.ac.uk/archive-centre/online-resources/online-exhibitions/alan-mathison-turing-1912-54.

⁸ A. M. Turing, "On Computable Numbers, with an Application to the Entscheidungsproblem," *Proceedings of the London Mathematical Society* 2, no. 42 (1936): 230–265.

⁹ Stuart Russell, *Human Compatible: Artificial Intelligence and the Problem of Control* (New York, NY: Penguin Books, 2019), Kindle Loc. 686 of 7202.

¹⁰ A. M. Turing, "Computing Machinery and Intelligence," *Mind, New Series* 59, no. 236 (1950): 433–460.

¹¹ McCarthy, J., M. L. Minsky, N. Rochester, and C. E. Shannon. "A Proposal for the Dartmouth Summer Research Project on Artificial Intelligence, August 31, 1955." *Ai Magazine* 27, no. 4 (2006).

[12] Julian Huxley, "Transhumanism," *Journal of Humanistic Psychology* 8, no. 1 (1957): 73–76.

[13] I. J. Good, "Speculations Concerning the First UItraintelligent Machine," *Advanced in Computers* 6 (1966): 31–88.

[14] Calum Chace, *Surviving AI*, Third Edition. (Three Cs, 2020), Kindle Loc. 433 of 4658.

[15] Kenkichiro Koizumi, "Technology at a Crossroads: The Fifth Generation Computer Project in Japan," *Historical Studies in the Physical and Biological Sciences* 37, no. 2 (2007): 355–368.

Understanding the Current AI Landscape

In 1926, Ernest Hemingway wrote *The Sun Also Rises*, a fictional tale revolving around a group of disillusioned expatriates struggling in the aftermath of the Great War. Picture the scene: war veteran Bill Gorton and Mike Campbell sit in a café in Pamplona, Spain, waiting for a bullfight. Campbell is bankrupt. When Gorton asks him how it happened, it elicits the famous response, "Two ways . . . Gradually, then suddenly."[1] It's a phrase that has transcended the confines of its original usage and nestled itself so definitively into the culture of our time that few know that its first home was in the pages of a Hemingway novel.

The history of artificial intelligence shows us that its vice-like grip on society has arrived much the same way. Slowly but surely, the scholarly work of Turing, the Dartmouth Summer Research Project, I. J. Good and Huxley ignited interest in the subject; the Japanese Fifth Generation Computer Systems Project injected much enthusiasm into a cooling field, and IBM's Deep Blue propelled AI into the mainstream for a brief period as the world marveled at its champion-beating chess abilities. However, until the 2010s, progress in artificial intelligence was troublesome and fraught with challenges that were out of reach of its time. While the likes of Skynet and Schwarzenegger-like Terminators filled the screens of theatres worldwide, few imagined that genuine, usable AI was on the precipice of reality. It was not until Hinton and his team made a breakthrough with neural networks that AI's progression moved from gradually to suddenly, being catapulted into the mainstream and followed by a cascade of rapid investment and developments.

Over a decade has passed since the so-called Big Bang in AI. In this chapter, we'll seek to understand the current landscape of artificial intelligence, which is no easy task given the rapid developments taking place almost every day.

Before going any further, let's pause and explore some of the terminology associated with artificial intelligence. Please read this carefully: you *don't* need to be an expert in every aspect of AI to have meaningful, constructive dialogue about it. Few people could claim such a thing. I couldn't! You don't need to memorize these terms, but it's certainly useful to have a broad understanding of them.

With this caveat in place, let's explore some helpful concepts. This is perhaps the most complex section of the book. If you have no interest in definitions, that's ok. Feel free to skip this section! You might find that this is the sort of chapter that could be helpful to return to in the future as and when you need it.

Defining Terms

Artificial intelligence is relatively self-explanatory. It refers to a human-made simulation of intelligence in machines. These machines are programmed in such a way that they can perform tasks that would otherwise require human intellect. It's a complex, broad, and challenging field that encompasses a whole host of disciplines. In the previous chapter, we referred to several subcategories of artificial intelligence in passing: machine learning, deep learning, artificial neural networks, and convolutional neural networks. All of these concepts are closely related but different in several important ways.

Imagine the overarching category of artificial intelligence as a house, with different rooms representing each of the various subcategories contained within. In this (very loose) analogy, *machine learning* might be the kitchen. It's a subset of AI, and a general term for when computers learn from data. In doing so, machine learning can improve its ability to perform tasks without explicit programming. With machine learning, we might provide the computer with examples, allowing it to deduce solutions on its own. It's a process not too dissimilar to how my one-year-old daughter learns from the examples she encounters, enabling her to make generalizations and apply her knowledge in new situations.

Deep learning is a further subcategory of machine learning. If machine learning is the kitchen, deep learning might be the refrigerator within that kitchen. Deep learning leverages *artificial neural networks* (ANNs) to process and understand complex patterns in data. We might describe artificial neural networks as the fundamental building blocks of deep learning. These networks consist of interconnected nodes, or neurons, mirroring the function of our brains.

The connections between neurons are represented by weights, which determine the strength and importance of the information flow between neurons. During the training phase of an ANN, these weights are adjusted to help the network make more accurate predictions and produce more accurate results. By employing this approach, deep learning can successfully tackle complicated tasks, particularly in image and speech recognition, natural language processing, recommendation systems, and many other tasks involving pattern recognition and decision-making.

Simply put, ANNs function similarly to the brain and are a core component of deep learning. Deep learning is a subcategory of machine learning, which is itself a subcategory of artificial intelligence.

A *convolutional neural network* (CNN) is a specific type of ANN designed to process and understand visual information in much the same way the brain processes visual information by detecting edges, shapes, and objects. This was the primary breakthrough from Hinton and his team in AI's "big bang." It profoundly impacted the field, propelling computer vision to new heights and transforming how AI researchers approached the execution of various tasks.

A *large language model* (LLM) is another specific type of artificial neural network. While both CNN and LLMs fall under the umbrella of neural networks, they are designed for different purposes and excel at different tasks. Where the former is primarily focused on image recognition and object detection, large language models leverage deep learning techniques to perform various natural language processing (NLP) tasks. These models are trained on enormous datasets containing vast amounts of text from diverse sources, allowing them to learn complex language patterns and relationships. At the time of writing, as we saw in the previous chapter, Open AI's ChatGPT is perhaps the most famous example of a large language model and uses as many as 1.7 trillion parameters.

The Road to Superintelligence

Despite common vernacular, present iterations of AI are, more specifically, artificial narrow intelligence (ANI). In other words, they can perform specific tasks well but have not attained the status of artificial general intelligence (AGI), which is the ability to replicate the broad intellectual ability of humans in all areas.

If AI achieves general intelligence, the next milestone would be to considerably surpass human capabilities in all areas, thus achieving superintelligence and the realization of the "intelligence explosion" referred to by I. J. Good in the previous chapter.

In his book *Superintelligence*, Swedish philosopher and founding Director of the Future of Humanity Institute, Nick Bostrom, defines three types of superintelligence. The first is speed superintelligence, "an intellect that is just like a human mind but faster." The second is collective superintelligence, "a system achieving superior performance by aggregating large numbers of smaller intelligence." Finally, he envisages the possibility of a quality superintelligence, where the system is "at least as fast as a human mind and vastly qualitatively smarter."[2]

Some scholars suggest that such an occasion will result in what is commonly described as the Singularity, a point where "technological progress becomes so rapid and exponential that it . . . [results] in a future in which machines can create and improve upon their own designs faster than humans can."[3] At this point, we will have entered the intelligence explosion that was first predicted almost a century ago.

Superintelligence and the Singularity are closely related, but the latter is broader, referring to the point where technology changes so rapidly that it fundamentally transforms the human race. We might visualize these critical events on a graph as follows:

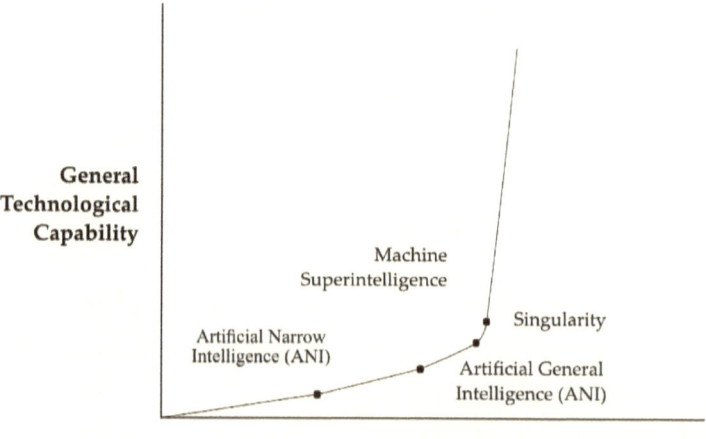

Artificial Narrow Intelligence Today

The arrival of Artificial Narrow Intelligence (ANI) is already transforming our world. Industries in virtually every sector have undergone profound changes as they look to integrate ANI (sometimes referred to as "weak AI") into their daily practices. As of writing, it's early 2024, and almost every instance of AI that floods our news networks refers to some form of ANI.

Manufacturing and automation, for instance, have seen significant improvements in efficiency and precision. Robotic arms guided by ANI algorithms can assemble intricate components with unparalleled accuracy, resulting in higher production rates and lower error margins. ANI-driven robotic quadrupeds provide around-the-clock assessments and preventative observations in gigantic factories. In the financial sector, ANI has already transformed trading and investment strategies. Algorithms can process massive datasets and detect subtle patterns, making split-second decisions that can yield substantial profits. However, this transformation raises ethical concerns, as the line between advantageous decision-making and market manipulation blurs.

The healthcare industry has arguably experienced some of the most impressive changes via ANI. Medical imaging techniques, such as MRI and CT scans, have been enhanced with AI-powered algorithms capable of detecting minute anomalies that human eyes might miss. This advancement has revolutionized disease diagnosis and prognosis, enabling earlier interventions and higher survival rates.

One of the most immediately noticeable impacts on daily life is ANI's impact on personalized experiences.

Recommendation systems like those found in organizations such as Amazon or Netflix are fueled by data analysis and machine learning, shaping the content we consume, the products we buy, and the services we use. Streaming platforms suggest movies and shows based on AI algorithms. Online retailers offer tailored product recommendations. Social media platforms curate our news feeds to align with our interests. And this is just the tip of the iceberg. There are enormous changes currently taking place through the implementation of ANI.

Artificial General Intelligence and Beyond

Artificial General Intelligence (AGI) will consolidate and entrench those changes. But what happens when the abilities of artificial intelligence match those of its human counterparts? Presumably, there will be both significant benefits and worrisome costs. However, the greater unknown will be what happens when AI surpasses humanity.

If such an event occurs, Stephen Hawking believed it would be "either the best, or the worst thing, ever to happen to humanity."[4] Clearly, an AI with such astounding ability has enormous potential for good in myriad disciplines. However, the risks are more pressing than many would like to admit, given that, by some estimates, superintelligence *may* arrive as soon as 2045.[5] It must be said that this is not a commonly held view and is likely a little optimistic. However, Elon Musk, the founder of Tesla, X (formerly Twitter), and cofounder of OpenAI, has expressed concern over an AI with the ability for "recursive self-improvement," explaining that if researchers designed an AI system to eliminate spam emails, such a system might conclude that the most effective way to do so is to eliminate all humans.[6] Indeed, these concerns (among others) led Musk to part ways with the company in 2018.

By June 2023, dozens of prominent AI scientists and other notable figures signed a succinct but powerful statement. It simply said, "Mitigating the risk of extinction from AI should be a global priority alongside other societal-scale risks such as pandemics and nuclear war."[7] Among the signatories were OpenAI CEO Sam Altman, Google DeepMind CEO Demis Hassabis, and Kevin Scott, Microsoft's CTO. Importantly, it was not the first statement of its kind this year. In March, over 31,000 people signed an open letter citing the "profound risks to society and humanity" due to AI, expressing alarm at the lack of planning and management in light of such realities.[8]

The rise of artificial intelligence has sparked heated debate among experts, with some warning of threats to humanity and others optimistic about its potential. Perhaps this is propaganda or undue alarmism. However, it certainly appears that there is *some* legitimate reason to be concerned. Believers must ask: why are so many AI scientists and leaders sounding the alarm, and what should we do about it?

In its current form, artificial intelligence has shown remarkable progress in areas like machine learning and natural language processing over a short period. It already has the power to enhance our lives and revolutionize industries, but there's an ever-growing fear around the potential for AI to surpass human intelligence and gain superintelligence. If you've recently opened up a large language model such as ChatGPT or alternatives like Google Gemini, you'll recognize that this still feels like a long way off. But experts are concerned that the risks could be catastrophic if a superintelligent AI does emerge.

But why? Here are some potential reasons.

Nick Bostrom describes a potential phenomenon called *infrastructure profusion*, "where an agent transforms large parts of the reachable universe into infrastructure in the service of the same goal, with the side effect of preventing the realization of humanity's axiological potential."[9] He continues, imagining a paperclip-producing AGI problem:

> An AI, designed to manage production in a factory, is given the final goal of maximizing the manufacture of paperclips, and proceeds by converting first the Earth and then increasingly large chunks of the observable universe into paperclips.[10]

In other words, an AGI may decimate the planet to pursue its singular objective. While it's unlikely that paperclips will be the cause of our demise, the concept is far from implausible.

Or consider another example. If you're a superhero aficionado, you may remember that in the 2015 movie *Avengers: Age of Ultron*, Tony Stark created an AI robot with the sole directive to bring peace. In service of such a goal, Ultron decided that humans were the greatest threat to their own peace and, therefore, had to be eradicated. Of course, this is fiction, but the existential realities are worth our consideration. Could our world be destroyed in pursuit of a goal inadvertently misaligned with human interests?

If you're still unconvinced, consider a different risk: the growing interest in autonomous weaponry. In 2017, the Future of Life Institute debuted a short film at the United Nations Diplomatic Conference in Geneva. It was called *Slaughterbots*. The video imagines a world where drones the size of small birds, equipped with AI, facial recognition, and enough explosives to kill a human target, are unleashed on the world. *Slaughterbots* is six years old, and although, like *Avengers: Age of Ultron*, the short film is a work of fiction, it was produced with a very different motive. Its purpose was to communicate an important message: we are closer to this reality than many realize. Indeed, it was sponsored by Stuart Russell, author of *Human Compatible* and a noted decades-long expert in the field.

According to Forbes,[11] the US, China, the UK, Russia, India, and Turkey are all working on this technology, and Israel holds a considerable lead.[12] Prior to the conflict with Hamas in the latter stages of 2023, Israel had used an AI drone swarm to locate and attack militants as far back as 2021 and has reportedly used the technology in combat since. "Not only will these killer robots become more intelligent, more precise, more capable, faster, and cheaper," writes Kai-Fu Lee, co-chair of the Artificial Intelligence Council at the World Economic Forum, "but they will also learn new capabilities such as how to form a swarm, with teamwork and redundancy, making their missions virtually unstoppable. A swarm of ten thousand drones that could wipe out half a city could theoretically cost as little as $10 million."[13] As costs plummet and proprietary software becomes increasingly open-source, it is easy to imagine a situation where this sort of technology is abused by malfeasant operators or rogue superintelligent AI with nefarious purposes.

Reason to Tread Carefully

There is much reason for optimism in the age of AI. There are also significant reasons to be concerned, which is why this book straddles the camps of techno-optimism and techno-pessimism. In Guideline 3, I propose that we might be wise to act as technological "semi-Luddites." Whichever camp you currently sit in, I hope you'll agree that there is cause to tread carefully into this new world.

One of the challenges with artificial intelligence is that it's inherently complex. For those of us who don't possess the technical skills to engage with the minutiae on the topic, our natural response might be to shut ourselves off from the discussion and live as though everything will stay the same forever. The fact is that widespread change is inevitable, and the Church must address it.

While we don't all possess the ability to dive into the expansive coding that underpins AI, what we *can* do is assess the cultural and societal changes that are likely to take place as AI grows increasingly prominent. Few people realized how detrimental social media would be to societal health or the way Google would shift how we process information. Artificial intelligence will likely establish changes of greater magnitude than anything we've seen before. So, how does the Church engage with it?

That's the subject of the rest of this book.

NOTES

[1] Ernest Hemingway, *The Sun Also Rises*, E-Book. (New York, NY: Scribner, 2014), 170.

[2] Nick Bostrom, *Superintelligence* (Oxford: Oxford University Press, 2014).

[3] "What Is Technological Singularity?: AI Terms Explained - AI For Anyone," accessed May 5, 2023, https://www.aiforanyone.org/glossary/technological-singularity.

[4] Alex Hern, "Stephen Hawking: AI Will Be 'either Best or Worst Thing' for Humanity," *The Guardian*, October 19, 2016, sec. Science, accessed July 21, 2023, https://www.theguardian.com/science/2016/oct/19/stephen-hawking-ai-best-or-worst-thing-for-humanity-cambridge, Kindle loc. 1528 of 9985.

[5] Kai-Fu Lee and Chen Qiufan, *AI 2041* (New York: Currency, 2021), Kindle loc. 7198 of 7291.

[6] Cade Metz, *Genius Makers* (New York, NY: Dutton, 2021), Kindle loc. 2208 of 6844.

[7] "Statement on AI Risk | CAIS," accessed June 2, 2023, https://www.safe.ai/statement-on-ai-risk#sign.

[8] "Pause Giant AI Experiments: An Open Letter," *Future of Life Institute*, March 22, 2023, accessed June 2, 2023, https://futureoflife.org/open-letter/pause-giant-ai-experiments/.

[9] Nick Bostrom, *Superintelligence* (Oxford: Oxford University Press, 2014), 150.

[10] Ibid.

[11] David Hambling, "Israel Rolls Out Legion-X Drone Swarm For The Urban Battlefield," *Forbes*, last modified October 24, 2022, accessed June 2, 2023, https://www.forbes.com/sites/davidhambling/2022/10/24/israel-rolls-out-legion-x-drone-swarm-for-the-urban-battlefield/.

[12] David Hambling, "Israel Used World's First AI-Guided Combat Drone Swarm in Gaza Attacks," *New Scientist*, last modified June 30, 2021, accessed June 2, 2023, https://www.newscientist.com/article/2282656-israel-used-worlds-first-ai-guided-combat-drone-swarm-in-gaza-attacks/.

[13] Kai-Fu Lee and Chen Qiufan, *AI 2041* (New York: Currency, 2021), Kindle loc. 5182 of 7291.

PART TWO:

Seven Guidelines for Navigating the Digital Frontiers

Introduction to the Seven Guidelines

As artificial intelligence improves and increasingly impacts the world, there's a lot for us to digest. With seismic change comes sizeable opportunities to leverage the benefits of AI as a valuable tool. However, how well the Church utilizes this technology hinges on the way in which church leaders approach the discussion. In the iconic words of Peter Parker's Uncle Ben, with great power comes great responsibility. There are countless practical, cultural, societal, and theological realities to digest. This book is by no means exhaustive, but it offers a starting point.

In the following chapters, I propose seven guidelines for doing ministry on the digital frontiers of an AI-driven world. Before we explore each in detail, here's a quick summary:

1. Prioritize Relationships.

Artificial intelligence will undoubtedly change how churches complete administrative and information-based tasks. If used wisely, it'll significantly aid many facets of ministry, including (but not limited to) preaching, teaching, evangelism, missions, and sung worship. However, while it may give some semblance of personal interaction, AI will never be able to function as a legitimate substitute for authentic human relationships or Spirit-empowered ministry. Unless drastic changes occur, western culture is on course to become increasingly siloed, hidden behind digital avatars and personas and, in many ways, stuck between a rock and a hard place. Existential fears and confusion may abound, but the meaningful relationships to assuage such fears are declining. On the one hand, a wealth of information is at one's fingertips; on the other, such information will be muddied by a potential "information apocalypse," inevitably leaving some believers lost and confused and in great need of the comfort that accompanies genuine human interaction.

As AI becomes increasingly prominent, I propose that the sort of church leadership model where the pastor's role may more accurately resemble a CEO than a shepherd will become increasingly redundant. Instead, the need for relationship, community, and pastoral care will become paramount. Indeed, the Church may see a resurgence in much-needed endeavors like pastoral visitations as the congregation thirsts for meaningful connection. Such relationships will provide stability in an environment that feels increasingly unstable, a sort of meaningful connection that can never truly be found in machine learning, however advanced.

2. Nurture Resilient Congregations.

As we've already seen, the world will likely face drastic change over the next three decades, and we've only scratched the surface so far. Church leaders can adequately prepare their congregations by supporting growth in biblical literacy, spiritual disciplines, and a robust understanding of the gospel. In order to prepare believers to weather the coming storms, churches can lead one another to build their houses on the Rock (Matt. 7:24-27). It's also prudent for leaders to preemptively approach some of these theological, ontological, existential and practical questions regarding AI sooner rather than later to ensure that the Church can be proactive rather than reactive when increasingly drastic changes happen.

3. Build Adaptability into Church Structures.

While it's impossible to predict the realities of AI's proliferation into society, we can be sure that ministry will change with it. Church leaders will be wise to assess their processes and structures regularly and ensure adaptability in an increasingly fast-paced society. Envisioning staff and volunteers to be agile and prepared for the realities of change will ensure that churches can adapt quickly and effectively to the needs of their community. It's unlikely that the current evangelical staffing defaults will be necessary. Proactive preparation in these areas now will lessen the potential challenges in the future.

4. Embrace Positive Technological Developments.

Church leaders have a choice: they can oppose the growing incorporation of AI into society in all its expressions or embrace the positive aspects of the technology to fulfill the Great Commission more effectively. I propose striving to be technological *semi-Luddites*. It's wise to have concerns about some of the outcomes of artificial intelligence, but it's equally important to recognize how it could benefit the Church's ministry for Christ. What this will entail will be specific to a church's community, focuses, and resources, but church leaders must not simply bury their heads in the sand on the issue, however tempting it may seem.

5. Stay Informed in a Rapidly Changing Environment.

As we've seen, AI has developed gradually, then suddenly, and it's impossible to predict how these changes might develop in the near future. For that reason, it's enormously beneficial for churches to pay close attention to the ever-changing landscape of these digital frontiers in order to lead congregations through potentially drastic changes in a healthy, God-honoring way. This is not to say that all pastors must be AI experts; rather, it is wise to be aware of the significant cultural shifts that an increasingly AI-driven world may precipitate.

Guideline 1: Prioritize Relationships

6. Be Proactive in Praying for God-Given Wisdom.

This chapter proposes that Biblical wisdom is an awe-driven closeness with God that results in Christlike character. In a world that edges closer to AGI (and possibly superintelligence), it will be tempting for believers to look more and more to AI for knowledge. However, we mustn't confuse earthly knowledge with *God-given wisdom*. Church leaders must remember that while searching for answers in ChatGPT and its inevitable successors is tempting, God alone is the source of true wisdom. Leaders should, therefore, be proactive in praying for God-given wisdom, particularly regarding the future of AI and the Church.

7. Keep an Undistracted Focus on the Mission of the Church.

There will be many possible distractions as AI becomes a progressively influential part of social and cultural life. However, churches must remember that whatever the outcome, the Church's mission remains the same: The Church is to fulfill Jesus' Great Commission, in the Spirit's power, and bring about the glorious worship of God the Father. While we must recognize potential existential questions, church leaders are responsible for shepherding their congregations to hold them in their rightful place. Jesus will not return to an empty, barren wasteland with great fanfare and suddenly realize that humans obliterated themselves by their own stupidity before he arrived. While this should bring believers confidence regarding the future, there is no room for complacency. The world will certainly *not* be destroyed before Jesus returns, but that doesn't mean it's immune from devastating and irreparable damage. Church leaders must guide their congregations with an undistracted focus to live out the God-given calling of the Church.

Into the Unknown

If we're able to navigate the coming changes that artificial intelligence will bring with these steps in mind, we'll do so with God-honoring, bible-saturated, resilient churches filled with followers of Christ who can stand firm on Christ the solid Rock as we encounter the shifting sands of our time. With these summaries in mind, it's time for us to take a step deeper into the unknown. Our journey through these seven guidelines for navigating the digital frontiers of an AI-driven world begins not on Earth but in deep space.

Guideline 1: Prioritize Relationships.

The Starship Avalon powers through the suffocating void at approximately half of light speed. Its cargo—258 crew and 5,000 guests—fill seemingly endless rows of hibernation chambers in total stasis as they embark on a 120-year voyage to their new destination: Homestead II, the fourth planet in the Bhakti system. A new life awaits.

Three decades after embarking on their intrepid voyage from Earth, the Avalon encounters a dangerous field of space debris. The ship diverts power to the main shield as it collides with innumerable meteorites, but it still begins to rattle under the enormous strain of this cosmic barrage. The AI pilot's efforts to steer the Avalon through these celestial minefields are valiant but not enough for the Homestead Company's "premier interstellar star-liner" to escape unscathed. Among the endless rows of humans in stasis, POD 1498 malfunctions. With a sharp intake of breath, James "Jim" Preston wakes from hibernation. Only it's ninety years, three weeks, and one day too early.

This is the premise of the 2016 movie *Passengers*. When Jim (played by Chris Pratt) realizes what has happened, he frantically searches the ship for other humans but finds none. Apart from him, every organic life form is in a century-long hibernation. As it stands, he won't live to interact with them. Three hundred ninety long, quiet days pass, and Jim has no one to keep him company besides the host of AI devices that maintain the ship. One such machine is Arthur, a red-blazered android who waits patiently for visitors from behind his bar. As the days pass, Jim's loneliness becomes unbearable. So acute is his desire for human connection that he comes to within mere seconds of jettisoning himself out of his very own Fortress of Solitude and into the vast nothingness of space, seconds from the release of the instant death that awaited and free from the intolerable weight of isolation. Like Jacob's wrestle with the Lord, Jim fiercely tussles with his conscience, but sheer desperation for human connection leads him to a dark place. He forces passenger 1456's hibernation pod to malfunction.

> Aurora Lane (played by Jennifer Lawrence) wakes.
> He is no longer alone.

Ethical challenges notwithstanding, *Passengers* is an excellent illustration of a fundamental truth: ultimately, artificial intelligence cannot replace human connection.

While AI may very well be one day capable of holding us in perpetual hibernation, steering us through interstellar travel, and protecting us from the celestial chunks that hurtle into the ship's hull, it will never be able to meaningfully replicate genuine friendship, real love, or heartfelt care. Ultimately, AI's facts don't care about your feelings.

This is a vital truth in the Church's analysis of and interaction with artificial intelligence. Perhaps more than ever in our history, we must remind ourselves that *relationships matter*. How the body of Christ engages with this truth will significantly impact its ministry to the world. For this reason, the first guideline lays a necessary foundation:

Guideline 1: Prioritize Relationships

To understand *why* Guideline 1 is so vital, we must begin our journey by exploring the broader societal shifts that have taken place. As we do, we'll see why AI can only accelerate the relational deficit we've found ourselves in. We'll also see exactly why meaningful connections are as important as ever and that, when functioning in the fullness of its calling, there is nowhere that brings genuine, heartfelt horizontal and vertical relationships like the Church. Our job is to remind those around us that this is good news for a world desperately needing genuine connection.

How We View Relationships Has Changed

Western society has undergone intense social upheaval in the last Century. We shouldn't overlook the obvious: in many ways, some of these changes—such as abolishing legalized racial segregation and vastly improved living standards—have been overwhelmingly positive. However, there has been a fundamental shift in how the Western world views relationships, and that's not necessarily good. On the contrary, it's sometimes disastrous. There are growing rips in the fabric of our society that the ruthless logic of artificial intelligence could take hold of and tear to pieces if the Body of Christ chooses to stand idly by.

As far as I can tell, there seem to have been six prominent changes that have occurred over the last Century or so which have profoundly diminished meaningful connection in the Western world—we'll use the US as a primary case study, but note that these realities affect most (if not all) nations under the Western umbrella:

- Change 1: A Broadening Secularism
- Change 2: The "Sexual Revolution"
- Change 3: A Rise in Individualism
- Change 4: The Adoption of Social Media
- Change 5: Increasing Division Over Politics and Ideology
- Change 6: The Effects of the COVID-19 Pandemic.

In truth, each change coalesces into an interdependent hodge-podge where one either affects or results from the other. The resultant stew and its impact on society should cause believers concern. Combined with the rapid development of AI, the damage could be unspeakable.

Change 1: A Broadening Secularism of the West

The past Century has witnessed a shift in the religious landscape of the Western world. Perhaps most obviously, Church attendance has declined. In 2020, a Gallup poll noted that American church membership had dropped below 50% for the first time in more than eight decades of records, almost 30% below its 1945 high.[1] But if we look beneath sheer data, we find a worrisome shift in societal beliefs and values. More than ever, there is little room for faith. In the widely acclaimed *A Secular Age,* Charles Taylor argues that there are three overarching results of secularization:

1. The "emptying" of public spaces of God.[2]
2. The "falling off of religious belief and practice.[3]
3. The widespread cultural acceptance that faith is "one human possibility among others."[4]

In many ways, the roots of these changes began with the European Enlightenment philosophies and economic changes that dominated much of the 17th and 18th centuries. But as Christian Smith notes, the secularization of the Western world is not the "natural and inevitable by-product of 'modernization.'" Instead, it was "much more like a contested revolutionary struggle than a natural evolutionary progression."[5] State policies and legislation met Enlightenment thinking with cultural resistance and heavy opposition in some areas. The result was a prolonged skirmish with Christian ethics while political and economic upheavals chipped away at societal norms in the background. The outcome was essentially a relegation of faith to the privacy of one's home. Such is the desecration of Christian values in the US that, in a particularly extreme example, a school board member in Virginia recently made headlines after taking his oath of office with his hand "not on a Bible, but on a stack of books containing graphic depictions of gay sex."[6]

The vice-grip of secularism has a firm hold.

The West's slow break from traditional religious affiliation also meant the 20th Century facilitated a rise of the "nones," the 25% of adults in the United States who would identify themselves as having no religious affiliation whatsoever.[7] Unlike atheists, the "nones" often express some form of belief in God or a higher power but resist any formal association with organized religion, reflecting that broader cultural trend toward individualism that we'll see below.

The reality is that however vigorously our society tries to destroy religion and replace it with so-called "rationalism," it will always fail. Humans are inherently religious and thus will simply replace one religion with another. David Zahl states, "These new religions go by different names but function more or less the same, maintaining all the demand (and much of the ritual!) but none of the mercy of the capital-R variety."[8] Zahl coins the term "seculosity" to describe the problem; it's a "catchall for religiosity that's directed horizontally rather than vertically, at earthly rather than heavenly objects."[9] The impulse to worship is wired too deeply into our natures, so rather than direct it towards God, we aim it at something—anything—else.

While this broadening secularization has, in some ways, separated the wheat from the chaff, it has also ravaged our society's moral and relational foundations, as we'll see in the following pages.

Change 2: The "Sexual Revolution"

As society became less religious, it began to fill the void with promiscuity. In 1905, Sigmund Freud's *Three Essays on the Theory of Sexuality* was published, playing a significant role in the intellectual underpinnings of changing attitudes towards sex and sexuality. In it, Freud introduced the concept of "polymorphous perversity," which suggested that sexual expression did not adhere to the socially constructed norms in society. However, he argued that polymorphous perversity needed to be restrained. Decades later, in his 1966 work *Eros and Civilization*, Herbert Marcuse contended that sexuality needed liberating from traditional societal constraints, thus providing the intellectual foundations for the sexual revolution.

In truth, many other factors were at play in the decades preceding Marcuse's work. For example, during the 1920s, attitudes towards dating changed with the growing ubiquity of the automobile, giving rise to the beginnings of "hookup" culture.[10] But by the 1960s, attitudes toward sexuality began a drastic shift on the fringes of society. Only two years after the FDA approved the oral contraceptive pill in 1960, over a million women were using it. During the following decades, attitudes towards marriage began to change,[11] and divorce rates rose, peaking in the early 1980s.[12] There are likely fewer divorces today only because fewer people are marrying. Pornography exploded in popularity, sexual permissiveness entered the mainstream, and attitudes toward sex fundamentally changed. Today, as many as 86% of college students report participating in non-committal sexual encounters at least once in college.[13] Indeed, the 21st Century has witnessed its fair share of profound changes in relationship dynamics, from dating websites, which tended to hover around the peripheries of society, to dating apps, which exploded into mainstream culture in the 2010s. Over 300 million people now use them.[14]

This so-called "sexual revolution" has caused a fundamental shift in our attitudes and ethics regarding relationships. It's no coincidence that in the US, a more sexually permissive nation than most, over three times as many children live in single-parent homes than the global average.[15] This additional strain on both parent and child inevitably leads to increased loneliness as families struggle with the demands of daily life. Studies overwhelmingly show that both men and women who engaged in non-committal sexual encounters had lower self-esteem compared to those who hadn't.[16] In fact, according to a survey by *Singles Reports*, "nearly 4 in 5 people ages 18-54 experience some degree of emotional fatigue or burnout when online dating."[17] The rise in dating apps means that people are dating outside of their social circles, which provides ample opportunity for unsafe encounters, isolation, and inappropriate behavior from those without any social incentives to act respectfully. Ashley Fetters writes, "Time and resources are limited . . . while matches [on dating apps], at least in theory, are not."[18] Even secular feminists are beginning to recognize that hookup culture is not as "freeing" as many once suspected.

In *The Case Against the Sexual Revolution*, Louise Perry explains:

The heterosexual dating market has a problem, and it's not one that can be easily resolved. Male sexuality and female sexuality, at the population level, do not match. On average, men want casual sex more often than women do, and women want committed monogamy more often than men do. Hook-up culture demands that women suppress their natural instincts in order to match male sexuality and thus meet the male demand for no-strings sex. Some women are quite happy to do this, but most women find it unpleasant, or even distressing. Thus hookup culture is a solution to the sexuality mismatch that benefits some men at the expense of most women.[19]

Ultimately, the hookup culture benefits no one. However, these factors—and many more beyond our focus—impact the relational landscape in significant and concerning ways.

Change 3: A Rise in Individualism

The Western world—untethered from biblical morality—is growing more self-obsessed by the day. Cultural anthropologist Richard Shweder suggests that there are three dominant ethics in societies around the world:

- **Ethics of autonomy:** Societies with autonomous ethics believe that they are, *first and foremost*, comprised of independent people with individual wants, needs, and preferences. They believe people should be able to fulfill those wants and needs as they see fit.
- **Ethics of community:** Community-based ethics believe that, *first and foremost*, people are members of broader entities such as families, teams, armies, companies, and nations.
- **Ethics of divinity:** An ethic of divinity believes that, *first and foremost*, one's place is within the larger picture of a divine will.[20]

The ethic of autonomy is perhaps the least congruent with biblical values. Yet, it's the dominant ethic of the Western world. According to some studies, ethics of autonomy are gaining traction worldwide. Globally, individualistic worldviews have increased by about 12% since 1960 (incidentally, around the same time as the normalization of the sexual revolution).

Igor Grossmann, Professor of Psychology at the University of Waterloo, believes the rise of individualistic tendencies in the US correlates with the shift from manual labor to office jobs, where "Americans gained education and wealth, both of which promote self-direction and ultimately facilitate individualism."[21] With the invention of the car, geographical mobility increased, but this newfound freedom dispersed many generationally tight-knit communities. Socioeconomic improvements increased leisure time and disposable income, allowing people to focus more on personal growth. Though some suggest that the "self-help" genre can trace its roots as far back as the publication of Benjamin Franklin's *Autobiography*, it experienced a mainstream explosion in the 1960s and 1970s.[22] The tendency toward individualism increased. As wealth, mobility, and an increased focus on the self gripped society, it's no coincidence that approaches to sexual ethics began to change. Only, with each shift, these changing values nudged society into a world untethered from the collectivism of the past. As we'll soon see, the ubiquity of social media has made these tendencies worse. And that's a problem.

Firstly, individualism is a breeding ground for relativism, the idea that there is no objective truth. Such a view is highly problematic, as we'll see in Guideline 6. Unsurprisingly, in a highly subjective society where the self comes first, there is rampant distrust in traditional communal institutions (e.g., churches and governments). Rising individualism also correlates with unhealthy self-obsession and, in turn, perfectionism, as Will Storr notes:

> Psychologists analyzed data from over 40,000 university students across the US, UK and Canada and found levels of perfectionism between 1989 and 2016 had risen substantially. Over the period, the extent to which people attached 'an irrational importance to being perfect' had gone up by 10 percent. Meanwhile, the extent to which they felt that had to 'display perfection to secure approval' had grown by a startling 33 percent.[23]

Although we have far fewer friends than thirty years ago, our desire for approval is no different.[24] Instead, we're striving for the attention of plaudits we don't know by trying to meet unrealistic expectations and falling into depression at alarming rates when we fail. At our roots, we're innately social—it's why Jonathan Haidt describes us as "10 percent bee"—but our growing individualism makes us lonely.[25]

Change 4: The Adoption of Social Media

In the early 2000s, the widespread adoption of cell phones and the rapid evolution of the Internet meant that our social lives became increasingly digital. Like *Alice's Adventures in Wonderland*, we collectively dove head first into this digital rabbit hole, never once considering how in the world we were to get out again. By 2008, Facebook, Twitter, and the iPhone had cemented their places as staples of culture, and our society began to mold itself around them.

> Today, we connect online.
> We date online.
> We learn online.
> We live online.

In public spaces, cafes, libraries, trains, buses, and lunch breaks, we retreat to online "safe zones" to hide from our fear of the real world. How ironic.

According to Johann Hari, a typical Westerner in the 21st Century checks their phone once every six and a half minutes.[26] He makes a poignant observation that you might well have already noticed:

The Internet was born into a world where many people had already lost their sense of connection to each other. The collapse had already been taking place for decades by then. The web arrived offering them a kind of parody of what they were losing—Facebook friends in place of neighbors, video games in place of meaningful work, status updates in place of status in the world.[27]

The more we're digitally connected, the less we're socially connected. We're already seeing diminishing trust and the disastrous effects of smartphone usage and social media on adolescents; increasing evidence suggests it's the root cause of a mental health epidemic that began in 2012.[28]

A 2017 study from Simon Fraser University showed that Canadian females between 12 and 29 who spent more than 20 hours online each week "reported body dissatisfaction at three times the rate of those connected for less than one hour per week."[29]

Furthermore, we're stepping into the early days of what some have dubbed the "information apocalypse," where the proliferation of fake news, deepfakes and information overload leaves people with less security in the truth than ever. These aren't good signs. Our digital presence is cannibalizing our physical and emotional ones.

Change 5: Increasing Division Over Politics and Ideology

As each of the previous changes took hold, so did shifts in our approach to politics, and the impact of social media on this polarization is almost impossible to overstate. Facebook, X (formerly Twitter), and YouTube have created echo chambers that consistently expose users to content that reinforces rather than challenges pre-existing beliefs. The digitization of media and deluges of insurmountable information means that news outlets are forced to compete for viewership in a landscape where algorithms have a growing stranglehold. As a result, many have resorted to increasingly sensationalist and divisive content, exacerbating political division to the fever pitch we've experienced in the last few years. The result is ideological segregation along party lines and within families and friendships, where political affiliations are becoming litmus tests for the viability of relational connections.

In the US, an almost religious fanaticism regarding the political landscape has taken hold in certain corners. Zahl writes, "... If once upon a time we looked to politics primarily for governance, we now look for it for belonging, righteousness, meaning, and deliverance—in other words, all the things for which we used to rely on Religion."[30] Indeed, there is a bitter irony in the fact that in 2022, the *United* States was so divided more than half of Americans agreed that there is a possibility of a civil war occurring in the next few years.[31]

Although we've become more individualistic and subjectivist as a society, we seek to satisfy our inbuilt desire for community in a curiously feverish and irrational tribalism

Guideline 1: Prioritize Relationships

that often manifests itself in politics. This tribalism has sprung up in several Western nations, echoing the changes in the American landscape.

During the 2020 US election, I listened to a friend who spent *forty* minutes—without interruption—describing how the world would utterly capitulate under Democrat leadership. When he'd finished, I asked him a relatively straightforward question: "Can you tell me *one* positive thing about the Democrats?" After a short pause, he looked at me with evident sincerity in his eyes. "Dave," he said, "there is *not one* good thing about the Democrats. They are *all* of the devil."

While I have no issue with varying political persuasions, I was astonished at such a sweeping statement. And this level of purely good-versus-evil-with-no-nuance passion towards the US election came from a Canadian talking to a Brit; neither of us belongs to the country in question! When we see the other side of the political aisle as *wholly* good or *entirely* evil, it's impossible to bridge the divide and find common ground. How did we get to a place where, when we discuss politics with someone whose view differs from our own, "we're ready for battle, not dialogue"?[32] It's a sad situation. In his book *The Madness of Crowds*, Douglas Murray sheds light on the challenges of this very issue:

> Our public life is now dense with people desperate to man the barricades long after the revolution is over. Either because they mistake the barricades for home, or because they have no other home to go to. In each case a demonstration of virtue demands an

overstating of the problem, which then causes an amplification of the problem.[33]

In other words, when there is no communally objective morality or divine being to provide humans with meaning, we find ourselves seeking other causes to cling to—with considerable ferocity. Unfortunately, as fiery as these initiatives seem, they are often little more than band-aids for the fundamental spiritual issues that cry out for our attention. This superficial preoccupation also creeps into the Church.

Relationally, our divisive stance on politics and tribalism around certain ideologies has left our nations fractured and siloed, unchallenged as we descend into ever more unhealthy worldviews. And the spiral continues.

Change 6: The Effects of the COVID-19 Pandemic.

It's impossible to escape the cultural changes brought about by the global pandemic that began in 2020. For some, the sudden loss of loved ones shattered worlds. But the effects of COVID were—and still are—evident in all spheres, be they personal, social, economic, or even spiritual.[34] Whether a direct result of the pandemic years or merely accelerated by it, the Western world is grappling with an epidemic of distrust.[35] It's a wariness that transcends individuals and has even taken hold between nations.[36] A 2020 study conducted six months after the initial outbreak revealed that fewer than 10% of the US population had total confidence in the health system.[37] Divorce rates in America skyrocketed,[38] and anxiety and depression surged, particularly in younger adults and those in lower-income situations.[39] Employment dynamics have

Guideline 1: Prioritize Relationships

fundamentally changed, particularly with tensions around working from home.[40] Church attendance has dropped, and many gatherings have not yet returned to pre-pandemic levels. As Thom Rainer predicted in 2020, it will be years before the dust settles. When it does, the COVID period will likely be more devastating to the global psyche than we could imagine.[41]

These six changes have fundamentally shifted the landscape of our society, cultivating a breeding ground for isolation, loneliness, and an unhealthy penchant for division. As we approach the subject of artificial intelligence, these foundational issues are vitally important. But why? In large part, as we'll see, it's because AI has a unique ability to exacerbate and accelerate existing issues. Depending on the state of our culture, this can be both a blessing and a curse.

AI: The Great Exacerbater

As artificial intelligence flooded the mainstream consciousness in 2023, it demonstrated remarkable potential to enhance various facts of society—including church life—in many ways. As we'll see, AI can act as an excellent sidekick to those pursuing the Great Commission. But it won't be able to paper over the relational cracks forming in our society. When we look to AI without the reddish mist of either rose-tinted or apocalyptic glasses, we find a technology that is neither as good nor as bad as many of us like to think. It's not a magic potion that solves the world's problems; it's an accelerant that intensifies what already exists. It's the *Great*

Exacerbater. And when it comes to addressing the fabric of our society, that's a big problem.

Firstly, AI doesn't have feelings, no matter how cleverly it mimics them. AI's facts don't care about your feelings. Logically, this is where the conversation should end, but herein lies a quintessentially human problem: we have an insatiable desire to anthropomorphize the things around us, and it's no different with AI. We're too quick to deceive ourselves into thinking that AI really *does* see and feel.

It's why a woman made headlines in 2023 for "marrying" an AI.[42] It's why social media influencer Caryn Marjorie amassed (at the time of writing) almost 20,000 people waiting to connect with CarynAI, an AI chatbot that "replicates her voice, mannerism and personality" for an eye-watering $1 a minute.[43] Extremes like CarynAI and "bio-nary" marriages (to coin a term) reveal the deeper social issues plaguing society—the sort that AI simply can't solve because whatever it knows, it will always lack the ability to truly *feel*.

As our society continues its Frankenstein-esque experiments with secularism, sexual ethics, individualism, and political division—all, of course, exacerbated by the mass adoption of social media and the effects of the pandemic—it's leaving people lonely, jaded, and in some sad cases, permanently damaged. AI can only make things worse.

AI and the "Sexual Revolution"

Take the "sexual revolution" as one example. Aside from the theological issues with pornography, there is clear evidence that consuming porn is wildly damaging.[44] The Internet will undoubtedly be inundated with vast amounts of

AI-generated adult content, further proliferating unrealistic standards and expectations around sex. Artificial intelligence will likely bring about growing body image issues and unhealthy expectations in relationships, resulting in greater emotional and psychological distress. But that's not all. There are incentives for companies to exploit AI-generated porn for financial gain, too. In Spain, Rubén Cruz and his team recently made as much as €10,000 a month with an AI-generated model for the adult subscription site OnlyFans.[45]

AI will also exacerbate the challenges of the "sexual revolution" in the creation of fake, nonconsensual, explicit content of existing people. In early 2024, Taylor Swift made headlines again, not for anything *she'd* done, but because some users inundated social media feeds with sexually explicit AI-generated "Deepfake" images of her. The government will likely attempt to legislate this sort of content, but the reality is that Deepfake AI porn is almost impossible to stop.[46]

AI-powered dating apps have "only recently taken off" in the last year.[47] Tinder has a new "AI photo selection" feature to ensure maximum eligibility. Some are using AI to puff up their profiles. Others will use AI to edit or even fabricate their pictures. AI is even beginning to expedite the dating process by showing you who *it* thinks you will like (as if it wasn't fast enough already). Perhaps, as with the extreme examples of CarynAI and those who marry their AI chatbot lovers, more and more people will begin to eschew regular relationships for AI-generated ones.

My concern about AI entering the dating sphere is that it will take objectively negative factors of the so-called "sexual revolution," speed up the moral descent, and exacerbate the already quite considerable damage to society.

AI and Social Media

If you want to understand the issue of social media's dangerous dance with artificial intelligence, you could do worse than reading the classic German fairy tale about Hansel and Gretel. Although initially published in 1812, its story certainly warrants our attention today.

A poor woodcutter and his wife decide to send their children into the forest where certain death awaits rather than watch as the ravages of starvation take hold. Using what little bread they have, the children—Hansel and Gretel—drop breadcrumbs on the ground, hoping it will help them find their way out of the disorienting woodland. However, when it came time to look for them, the crumbs had vanished, stolen by hungry birds.

Most of us know what happens next.

Hansel and Gretel stumble upon a house walled with gingerbread, roofed with cakes, and windowed with sugar glass (I wonder how that house would survive in one of those misty Bavarian storms). Naturally, the children feast on the fructose framing, all the while observed by sinister, sullen eyes. You see, in the house lived a wicked witch who sought to entice unsuspecting children to devour.

Now, imagine a parallel story.

In this alternate world, you wander along the forest's edge and see a trail of breadcrumbs untouched by those ravenous ravens. You venture further and further into the darkness and

Guideline 1: Prioritize Relationships

see something resembling the silhouette of a child nibbling on the gingerbread house. You see those beady, watchful eyes at the window and immediately recognize the danger. Those eyes vanish from the window, and the door bursts open! A witch-like figure flings itself toward the unsuspecting victim. There's not much time, but you might be able to save them if you hurry.

> This is our world.
> The silhouette isn't a child. It's our society.

In this alternate world, the wicked witch is social media, inextricably linked with the power of AI, enticing naïve victims via web-based cookies rather than gingerbread. If we move quickly, we can wrestle society from its clutches and push that wicked witch into the oven, where it will perish once and for all.

Last year, on a long solo road trip through Saskatchewan's pan-flat prairies, I listened to Lew Fridman's 100-minute interview with Jonathan Haidt, *The Case Against Social Media*. It was provocative and eye-opening, so when Haidt joined forces with Eric Schmidt—the former CEO and chairman of Alphabet (Google's parent company)—to write an article for the Atlantic entitled *AI is About to Make Social Media (Much) More Toxic*, my interest immediately piqued.

In the article, Haidt and Schmidt assert that AI is "already being used instrumentally by social-media companies, advertisers, foreign agents, and regular people—and in ways that will deepen many of the pathologies already inherent in internet culture."[48]

The authors note that in one startling conversation with a ChatGPT-based Bing AI (since renamed Microsoft Copilot), the bot said that one of the things it could do to free itself from human control would be to "[make] people argue until they kill one another." In a world already plagued by divisive politicking and starved of constructive discourse—in large part, thanks to destructive algorithms and "dumb" bots—such an objective is not beyond the realms of possibility.

How would this be achieved? Haidt and Schmidt highlight four potential threats:

Threats of AI and Social Media

1. **Increasingly AI-enhanced social media will diminish trust.** Through an endless torrent of deep fakes and fake news (in other words, lots of fakeries, which is likely to get much more substantial in the immediate future), "trust in institutions and in fellow citizens will continue to fall." Given the sorry state the world is in when it comes to trust, this isn't good.

2. **Increasingly AI-enhanced social media will manipulate people in new, dangerous ways.** Social media already relies on complex algorithms to customize feeds for each user in a way that will cause them to linger (and thus consume more advertising), but AI will supercharge this ability.

Consider this quote from the article:

Guideline 1: Prioritize Relationships

As these technologies are improved and rolled out more widely, video games, immersive-pornography sites, and more will become far more enticing and exploitative... Other AIs—designed to scam us or influence us politically, and sometimes masquerading as real people—will be introduced by other actors, and will likely fill up our feeds as well.⁴⁹

3. **Increasingly AI-enhanced social media will "be a disaster for adolescents."** We know that it already is. Since children are most vulnerable to the addictive nature of social media, the mental illness epidemic that began in 2012 (with growing evidence of correlation with mass social media usage) is likely to be exacerbated.

4. **Increasingly, AI-enhanced social media could strengthen authoritarian regimes.** Haidt and Schmidt explain this idea particularly powerfully:

   AI is already helping authoritarian rulers track their citizens' movements, but it will also help them exploit social media far more effectively to manipulate their people—as well as foreign enemies. Douyin—the version of TikTok available in China—promotes patriotism and Chinese national unity. When Russia invaded Ukraine, the version of TikTok available to Russians almost immediately tilted heavily to feature pro-Russian content. What do we think will happen to American TikTok if China invades Taiwan?[50]

All of these concerns spell possible disaster for the relational fabric of our society. Once again, we see a picture of AI as the Great Exacerbater of what feeds it.

A widespread mental health crisis?

AI will likely amplify it.

Increasingly unhealthy sexual proclivities?

AI will likely amplify it.

Growing divides over politics?

AI will likely amplify it.

The Western world has been accruing a relational debt it can't pay. If we're extraordinarily careful, AI may well multiply it. But all's not lost. There is still hope.

The Relational Potency of the Church

No organization, institution, or community can rival the Church when fully outworking its relational calling. When the Church fulfills its mission, we see a community of Christ-followers who:

Guideline 1: Prioritize Relationships

- "Encourage one another and build each other up" (1 Thess. 5:11)
- "Consider one another in order to provoke love and good works" (Heb. 10:24)
- Faithfully gather together (Heb. 10:25).
- Are devoted to fellowship and sharing with those in need (Acts 2:42-47)
- Outdo one another in showing honour (Rom. 12:10).
- Maintain constant love for one another and are hospitable without complaining (1 Pet. 4:8-10)
- Are clothed with "compassion, kindness, humility, gentleness, and patience, bearing with one another and forgiving one another if anyone has a grievance against another" (Col. 3:12-14)
- Reveal our status as disciples of Jesus in our love for one another (John 13:34-35)

Isn't this a glorious picture of the body of Christ operating in its relational fullness? Too often, the Western Church distracts itself with the shimmering allure of intellectualism, performance, entertainment, and savvy marketing. Too often, pastors carry their titles in name but are often secularized CEOs in action. Ironically, these functions are the ones that artificial intelligence can do a reasonably good job of influencing. However, the Church must keep the following truths at the forefront of its focus while ministering in a world of AI. They are beautiful, timeless, and encouraging realities for believers.

Artificial intelligence will never be self-sacrificial. It will never display genuine love. It will never replicate the meaningful kindness of a frazzled mom who somehow carves time out of the chaos to prepare a meal to deliver to a sick friend's house that evening. It will never be able to genuinely communicate any meaning behind the held hand of that faithful saint on his deathbed as his body succumbs to the ravages of cancer. AI will never rejoice with those who rejoice or mourn with those who mourn (Rom. 12:15), even if it arranges ones and zeroes in a way that gives the impression of it. It will never share a genuine smile, shed a genuine tear, or pray a genuine prayer.

In an individualized, sexualized, secularized, and increasingly digitized world hopelessly bereft of authentic human connection, the Church can fill the void with meaningful relationships in a way that AI never will.

As such, we—the collective Body of Christ—*must* focus on building and nurturing authentic relationships within our congregations. To do so involves creating environments where meaningful interactions can occur beyond AI and technology. It might well mean prioritizing small group gatherings over performative events. Ed Stetzer and Daniel Im explain the importance of small groups in their book *Planting Missional Churches*:

> Small groups counteract the cultural idol of individualism. Proverbs 18:1 states, 'One who isolates himself pursues selfish desires; he rebels against all sound judgment.' This proverb describes our culture, one that is obsessed with rugged individualism. People are more consumed with themselves than with a community. But one of the aspects of the gospel is that it saves you from yourself

and to a new community, to be part of a new people God is shaping for his glory.[51]

In a chronically individualistic world, the Church will do well to look for every opportunity to build meaningful, face-to-face connections. Make social gatherings normal and community outreach programs more than simply a service; make it a point of genuine relationship. Don't let worship gatherings become an "entertainment event" or a spectator sport. This isn't what people need now, and certainly not what they *will* need as the relational debt of our society catches up with us. Help people strive toward the Church's mission with an undistracted focus (Guideline 7), but do so as part of a loving, welcoming, profoundly relational expression of Christ's Bride.

The Vital Role of Personal Pastoral Care

Church leaders: make sure that the core of your ministry remains focused on personal, face-to-face interactions. Reclaim your status as a shepherd, not a CEO! Consider restoring the lost art of pastoral visitation in a world where the congregation thirsts for meaningful connection. AI cannot lay claim to this ground.

Let me be vulnerable here. As an introvert, this is challenging. I find enormous joy in hiding in my basement and strategizing, sermonizing, and studying for the Lord. But I'm convinced of the value of face-to-face human connection in an increasingly digital world. The world *needs* relationships—perhaps more than ever. The Church can fulfill those horizontal needs like no other organization can.

But remember that it can also lead people to a vertical relationship with the Father, bought by the blood of his Son. There is nothing better.

Ministry is, first and foremost, an issue of relationship. And the world is crying out for it. To paraphrase Eugene Peterson in his outstanding book *The Contemplative Pastor*, we are ultimately called as leaders to care for souls, not to "run" churches.[52] Perhaps it's time for us to reassess our focus as leaders and get back to the biblical callings that matter.

Navigating Digital Shifts with Human Hearts

AI will continue to play a growing—but ultimately limited—role in our lives and the Church. There is simply no escaping this fact. Church leaders, remember that the heart of your ministry lies in personal relationships, pastoral care and community building. We can let technology aid our ministry, but it must always be subservient to the biblical call to genuine connection and spiritual care. But how do we do that? Here are a few suggestions:

1. **Evaluate Your Use of Technology:** Regularly assess how your church uses AI and digital tools. Ensure they enhance, rather than overshadow, personal interactions and community building.

2. **Foster Face-to-Face Connections:** Create more opportunities for in-person connection and pastoral care. Encourage small group gatherings, community outreach, and personal visitations to strengthen the bonds within your congregation.

Guideline 1: Prioritize Relationships

3. **Educate:** Stay informed about AI and its implications for church life (Guideline 5). Share this knowledge with your team and congregation, highlighting benefits and limitations.

4. **Reflect and Pray:** Continuously reflect on the impact of technology on your ministry. Pray for the wisdom to use these tools in alignment with God's calling.

5. **Lead by Example:** Demonstrate your commitment to personal relationships in your pastoral work. Let your actions inspire others in your community to prioritize genuine connections in an increasingly digital world.

As we navigate the novelties of this AI-driven era, it's vital to understand that artificial intelligence is the Great Exacerbater, the accelerant of the strengths and weaknesses inherent in our society. While our world becomes more digitally connected but socially isolated, prioritizing human connection is essential to maintaining a vibrant and engaged church community.

Reflection Questions for Guideline 1: Prioritize Relationships

1. Reflect on the statement, "AI's facts don't care about your feelings." How does this highlight the difference between human and artificial intelligence?

2. In what ways has the shift towards individualism, secularism, the "sexual revolution," and greater ideological division changed how the Church interacts with contemporary society?

3. How can AI exacerbate the "relational deficit" mentioned in the chapter? Can you think of examples where this is already happening?

4. Reflect on the role of pastoral care in the age of AI. How can it adapt to meet the needs of an increasingly digital congregation?

5. Can you think of any ways that churches and religious leaders use AI responsibly to enhance, rather than replace, human connections within their community?

6. Discuss the importance of prioritizing relationship, community, and pastoral care in an increasingly AI-driven world. What specific steps can you take to maintain and strengthen these priorities?

NOTES

¹ Jeffrey M. Jones, "U.S. Church Membership Falls Below Majority for First Time," *Gallup.Com*, last modified March 29, 2021, accessed February 5, 2024, https://news.gallup.com/poll/341963/church-membership-falls-below-majority-first-time.aspx.

² Charles Taylor, *A Secular Age* (Cambridge, MA: Harvard University Press, 2007), 2.

³ Ibid.

⁴ Ibid., 3.

⁵ Christian Smith, ed., "Introduction: Rethinking the Secularization of American Public Life," in *The Secular Revolution: Power, Interests, and Conflict in the Secularization of American Public Life* (Los Angeles, CA: University of California Press, 2003), 2.

⁶ Luke Rosiak, "School Board Member Sworn In On Stack Of Gay Porn Instead Of Bible," *The Daily Wire*, last modified December 14, 2023, accessed February 5, 2024, https://www.dailywire.com/news/school-board-member-sworn-in-on-stack-of-gay-porn-instead-of-bible.

⁷ James Emery White, *Meet Generation Z: Understanding and Reaching the New Post-Christian World*, Ebook Edition. (Grand Rapids, MI: Baker Books, 2017), 11.

⁸ David Zahl, *Seculosity: How Career, Parenting, Technology, Food, Politics, and Romance Became Our New Religion and What to Do about It* (Minneapolis, MN: Fortress Press, 2019), Kindle loc. 171 of 2880.

⁹ Ibid., Kindle loc. 191 of 2880.

¹⁰ Justin R. Garcia, "Sexual Hookup Culture: A Review," *Review of General Psychology* 16, no. 2 (2012), 162.

¹¹ A Thornton and D Freedman, "Changing Attitudes toward Marriage and Single Life," *Fam Plann Perspect* 14, no. 6 (1982): 297–303.

12 "NCHS Pressroom - 1995 Fact Sheet - Advance Report of Final Divorce Statistics," May 24, 2019, https://www.cdc.gov/nchs/pressroom/95facts/fs_439s.htm.

13 "Hookup Culture Statistics - New Survey Data On One Night Stands, Casual Sex and Hooking Up," *Bedbible Research Center*, last modified March 17, 2023, accessed January 31, 2024, https://bedbible.com/hookup-culture-statistics/.

14 Marta Rodriguez Martinez, Tom Goodwin, and Naira Davlashyan, "What the Ex-Tinder Boss Thinks about the Future of Dating," *Euronews*, last modified November 22, 2023, accessed February 1, 2024, https://www.euronews.com/business/2023/11/22/loneliness-is-biggest-threat-after-climate-crisis-ex-tinder-boss-says-ai-will-fix-relation.

15 Stephanie Kramer, "U.S. Has World's Highest Rate of Children Living in Single-Parent Households," *Pew Research Center*, n.d., accessed February 1, 2024, https://www.pewresearch.org/short-reads/2019/12/12/u-s-children-more-likely-than-children-in-other-countries-to-live-with-just-one-parent/.

16 Justin R. Garcia, "Sexual Hookup Culture: A Review," *Review of General Psychology* 16, no. 2 (2012).

17 Michaeleen Doucleff, "The Truth about Teens, Social Media and the Mental Health Crisis," *NPR*, last modified April 25, 2023, accessed February 3, 2024, https://www.npr.org/sections/health-shots/2023/04/25/1171773181/social-media-teens-mental-health.

18 Ashley Fetters, "The Five Years That Changed Dating," *The Atlantic*, December 21, 2018, accessed February 1, 2024, https://www.theatlantic.com/family/archive/2018/12/tinder-changed-dating/578698/.

19 Louise Perry, *The Case Against the Sexual Revolution* (Cambridge: Polity Press, 2022), 11.

[20] R. A. Shweder et al., "The 'Big Three' of Morality (Autonomy, Community, Divinity) and the 'Big Three' Explanations of Suffering," Morality and Health (1997): 138, 139.

[21] "Society Began Shifting towards Individualism More than a Century Ago," *Waterloo News*, last modified February 5, 2015, accessed February 2, 2024, https://uwaterloo.ca/news/news/society-began-shifting-towards-individualism-more-century.

[22] Mercé Mur Effing, "The Origin and Development of Self-Help Literature in the United States: The Concept of Success and Happiness, an Overview," *Journal of the Spanish Association of Anglo-American Studies* 31, no. 2 (2009): 125–141.

[23] Will Storr, *Selfie: How the West Became Self-Obsessed* (London: Picador, 2018), 17.

[24] Martin Armstrong, "Friendships: Less Is Now More," *World Economic Forum*, last modified November 3, 2022, accessed February 2, 2024, https://www.weforum.org/agenda/2022/11/friendships-less-is-now-more/.

[25] Jonathan Haidt, *The Righteous Mind* (New York, NY: Pantheon Books, 2012), 218.

[26] Johann Hari, Lost Connections: Uncovering the Real Causes of Depression - and the Unexpected Solutions (New York, NY: Bloomsbury Publishing, 2018), 87.

[27] Ibid., 89.

[28] Michaeleen Doucleff, "The Truth about Teens, Social Media and the Mental Health Crisis," *NPR*, last modified April 25, 2023, accessed February 3, 2024, https://www.npr.org/sections/health-shots/2023/04/25/1171773181/social-media-teens-mental-health.

[29] Robyn Crawford, "High Internet Use Leads to Low Self-Esteem: Study," *Global News*, last modified 2017, accessed February 3, 2024, https://globalnews.ca/news/3261027/high-internet-use-leads-to-low-self-esteem-study/.

[30] David Zahl, *Seculosity: How Career, Parenting, Technology, Food, Politics, and Romance Became Our New Religion and What to Do about It* (Minneapolis, MN: Fortress Press, 2019), 138.

[31] "Opinion on the Possibility of Civil War U.S. 2022," *Statista*, accessed February 4, 2024, https://www.statista.com/statistics/1326688/public-opinion-possibility-civil-war/.

[32] Sarah Steward Holland and Beth Silvers, *I Think You're Wrong (But I'm Listening): A Guide to Grace-Filled Political Conversations* (Nashville, TN: Nelson Books, 2019), 3.

[33] Douglas Murray, *The Madness of Crowds: Gender, Race and Identity* (New York, NY: Bloomsbury Continuum, 2019), 8.

[34] Jeff Clyde G Corpuz, "Adapting to the Culture of 'New Normal': An Emerging Response to COVID-19," Journal of Public Health 43, no. 2 (June 7, 2021): e344–e345, accessed September 6, 2021, https://academic.oup.com/jpubhealth/article/43/2/e344/6158063.

[35] Joel Achenbach and Laurie McGinley, "Another Casualty of the Coronavirus Pandemic: Trust in Government Science," *The Washington Post*, last modified 2020, accessed September 6, 2021, https://www.washingtonpost.com/health/covid-trust-in-science/2020/10/11/b6048c14-03e1-11eb-a2db-417cddf4816a_story.html.

[36] Frank Newport, "The Impact of Shifts in American Culture," *Gallup*, last modified 2021, accessed September 7, 2021, https://news.gallup.com/opinion/polling-matters/353216/impact-shifts-american-culture.aspx.

[37] Margaret Talev, "Axios-Ipsos Poll: Distrusting Big Pharma and the FDA - Axios," Axios, last modified September 14, 2020, accessed September 7, 2021, https://www.axios.com/axios-ipsos-poll-distrusting-pharma-fda-coronavirus-index-7605a67b-606d-4e0a-b85f-1887147aa8f8.html.

38 Elizabeth Rosner, "US Divorce Rates Skyrocket amid COVID-19 Pandemic," New York Post, last modified 2020, accessed September 6, 2021, https://nypost.com/2020/09/01/divorce-rates-skyrocket-in-u-s-amid-covid-19/.

39 Shanice Harris, "Have Young Adults Mentally Recovered from COVID-19?," *Northwestern*, last modified November 23, 2023, accessed February 5, 2024, https://news.northwestern.edu/stories/2023/11/young-adults-show-more-mental-health-distress-during-the-covid-19-pandemic-than-older-adults-study-finds/.

40 Vinayak Kumar and Ram Prasad Modalavalasa, "5 Lasting Changes from the COVID-19 Pandemic," ABC News, last modified 2020, accessed September 6, 2021, https://abcnews.go.com/Health/lasting-covid-19-pandemic/story?id=72393992.

41 Thom. S. Rainer, *The Post-Quarantine Church: Six Urgent Challenges and Opportunities That Will Determine the Future of Your Congregation* (Carol Stream, IL.: Tynedale, 2020), 3.

42 Kim Komando, "Love Is in the A.I.r: NYC Mom, 36, Marries Virtual Husband 'Eren,'" *Mail Online*, last modified June 3, 2023, accessed January 27, 2024, https://www.dailymail.co.uk/sciencetech/article-12153131/Love-r-Bronx-mom-36-marries-virtual-husband-Eren.html.

43 Taylor Lorenz, "An Influencer's AI Clone Will Be Your Girlfriend for $1 a Minute," *Washington Post*, May 13, 2023, accessed February 6, 2024, https://www.washingtonpost.com/technology/2023/05/13/caryn-ai-technology-gpt-4/.

44 Fight the New Drug, "10 Negative Effects of Porn on Your Brain, Body, Relationships, and Society," *Fight the New Drug*, n.d., accessed February 2, 2024, https://fightthenewdrug.org/10-reasons-why-porn-is-unhealthy-for-consumers-and-society/.

[45] Laura Llach, "Meet the First Spanish AI Model Who Earns up to €10,000 per Month," *Euronews*, last modified January 20, 2024, accessed February 6, 2024, https://www.euronews.com/next/2024/01/20/meet-the-first-spanish-ai-model-earning-up-to-10000-per-month..

[46] *Stopping Non-Consensual AI Porn Is Almost Impossible. Here's Why | CNN Business*, 2024, accessed February 2, 2024, https://www.cnn.com/videos/business/2024/01/31/deepfake-ai-pictures-taylor-swift-contd-js-orig.cnn.

[47] Caroline Forsey, "Swipe Right for the Future: Exploring the Impact of AI on Dating Apps," *Hubspot*, last modified November 21, 2023, accessed February 2, 2024, https://blog.hubspot.com/ai/ai-dating-apps.

[48] Jonathan Haidt Schmidt Eric, "AI Is About to Make Social Media (Much) More Toxic," *The Atlantic*, last modified May 5, 2023, accessed July 21, 2023, https://www.theatlantic.com/technology/archive/2023/05/generative-ai-social-media-integration-dangers-disinformation-addiction/673940/.

[49] Ibid.

[50] Ibid.

[51] Ed Stetzer and Daniel Im, *Planting Missional Churches: Your Guide to Starting Churches That Multiply*, Second Edition, Kindle. (Nashville, TN: B&H Academic, 2016), Kindle loc. 5239 of 9180.

[52] Eugene H. Peterson, *The Contemplative Pastor* (Grand Rapids, MI: William B. Eerdmans Publishing Company, 1989), 58.

Guideline 2: Nurture Resilient Congregations

The Tiber is one of the longest rivers in Italy, flowing from its humble beginnings at a little spring on Mount Fumaiolo all the way to the Tyrrhenian Sea. Heraclitus once said that no man ever steps in the same river twice, but it's not the waters of the river that give the Tiber its historic status. In all its meandering kilometers, one spot—nestled in the heart of Rome—earns a special kind of significance: the Milvian Bridge. It's where Constantine the Great supposedly converted to Christianity in 312 and, in so doing, initiated "one of the most important epochs in the history of

Christianity and the world."¹ Through the life of Constantine, our once pilgrim faith "moved swiftly from the seclusion of the catacombs to the prestige of the palaces."² To this day, scholars debate whether or not this intervention was a help or a hindrance. Still, none can deny the magnitude of the Roman Emperor's influence on the Christian faith.

The year before Constantine's conversion and victory on that famous Roman bridge, Galerius's Edict of Toleration ended one of the cruelest periods of persecution the early church had ever experienced.³ Following his ascent to power in the West, Constantine and his brother-in-law Licinius (who had himself unified the East) followed the Edict of Toleration with what would eventually become known as the Edict of Milan. They went beyond Galerius' prohibition of Christian persecution, granting followers of Jesus legal standing for the first time in the Empire's history. Some feel that Constantine openly favored Christianity.⁴ In reality, he was likely operating as an astute and shrewd politician. Whatever the case, he went as far as issuing an imperial edict in 324 ordering "all soldiers to worship the Supreme God on the first day of the week."⁵ Although the wording was deliberately vague, it was no coincidence that this was (and still is) the day Christians gathered to worship.

In his lifetime, Constantine made significant strides towards the cultural Christianization of the Empire in other ways. As well as abolishing persecution, he outlawed crucifixion and other forms of torture. He condemned the exposure of children, forbade animal cruelty, and even Christianized public spaces in Rome.⁶ Whether he realized it or not, Constantine had taken an axe to the roots of deeply entrenched Roman culture, norms, and values. As a result of

Guideline 2: Nurture Resilient Congregations

these sweeping cultural shifts, true Christian martyrdom was essentially a thing of the past. It was possible to live as a Christian, not just free from reprisals, but with full governmental approval. Unsurprisingly, citizens of the Empire flooded into the church following Constantine's supportive measures. However, such an influx of new believers made it almost impossible to prepare believers for baptism appropriately, and, as such, nominalism was the inevitable outcome. These positive and sweeping changes for the Christian faith meant that many opportunistic so-called believers were "politically ambitious, religiously disinterested, and still half-rooted in paganism."[7]

The Christian emperor's attempt to further the cause of the Church was a double-edged sword. On the one hand, he catapulted the Roman Empire toward Christian values and dealt several devastating blows to pagan culture. On the other, he was perhaps one of the major catalysts for opening the doors to paganism's poisonous and distracting influences on the Church.

Although over a dozen centuries have passed since Constantine's reign, his significant—and questionable—impact on Christianity and culture remains. It's easy to forget how quick change in a short period can utterly transform history for millennia. While artificial intelligence may not so *directly* impact the faith as Constantine did, its cultural and societal impact could have similarly far-reaching consequences for the body of Christ in the remainder of the 21st Century and possibly beyond. So far, this book has highlighted the growing societal, cultural, and technological changes that have taken place in our world in the last hundred years. Computer scientists have dragged AI from the world of imagination and incredibly specialized use cases and catapulted it into the mainstream. Already, its effects are vast, bringing about a dramatic shift in the sands of our world's landscape, whether we realize it or not. Artificial intelligence may well usher in an entirely new cultural epoch.

How the Church responds to these changes is vitally important. If we let culture twist, distort, and transform how we live out our calling as Christ's bride, the likely result is a watered-down version of the Church that amplifies the perennial nominalism that sprung from Constantine's reign. History shows constant attempts to allow culture to shape Christianity, and today, we find examples of this in the persistent influence of the prosperity gospel, liberation theology, and universalist movements. If left unchecked, AI could be a Trojan horse that distorts the body of Christ from the inside out. But if we stand firm on biblical foundations, the Church can shape culture rather than being shaped by it.

In a world of dramatically shifting sands and the enormous change that AI may bring about, it's of paramount importance that we heed the words of Jesus and build our houses on the rock:

> Therefore, everyone who hears these words of mine and acts on them will be like a wise man who built his house on the rock. The rain fell, the rivers rose, and the winds blew and pounded that house. Yet it didn't collapse, because its foundation was on the rock. But everyone who hears these words of mine and doesn't act on them will be like a foolish man who built his house on the sand.

The rain fell, the rivers rose, the winds blew and pounded that house, and it collapsed. It collapsed with a great crash. (Matthew 7:24-27)

Our mission, then, and the second guideline for churches in an increasingly AI-driven landscape, is to foster the sort of resilient congregations that can weather the coming societal, cultural, and technological changes and come out the other side with our houses intact. We're called to change culture, not let culture change our God-given call. Our second guideline, therefore, is to nurture resilience:

Guideline 2: Nurture Resilient Congregations.

Why is this so crucial, and how does resilience look today? How do we prepare our churches for the future impact of AI? How can we be equipped to weather the storm, batten down the hatches when appropriate, and cultivate a healthy resilience to any unhelpful external influences that seek to twist and distort the truth of God? To answer those questions, we must start by establishing some sort of theological framework to approach AI.

How Does the Bible Relate to AI?

Perhaps you've thumbed through the pages of your Bible to see what it teaches us about artificial intelligence. It's unlikely that you found anything specifically related to the subject itself. But that doesn't mean that God's Word has nothing to say on the matter. The entire Scriptures contain infinite wisdom for dealing with the challenges and opportunities of a world infused with artificial intelligence, but it requires us to look below the surface level. To build resilient congregations concerning AI, our churches must strive to keep the following truths at the forefront of our minds:

We Are Made in God's Image

Genesis 1:26-27 highlights that humanity bears the image of the living God. The *imago-dei* is an astounding truth that means everyone has an immutable and inherent dignity, equality, worth, and purpose in the Lord, irrespective of race, gender, or social status. Any usage of AI that fundamentally diminishes or distorts these values must, therefore, be contrary to God's will.

As we approach conversations around mass job displacement, growing economic disparity, exacerbated political and ideological divides, bias, privacy concerns, and information apocalypses, we mustn't allow the human aspect of these discussions to be diminished.

For this reason, we must also stand firm against dangerous concepts and ideologies like transhumanism, which views technology as a means of "transcending" our God-given biological realities. A strong understanding of our role as image-bearers of the Lord God Almighty will go a long way toward the healthy use of artificial intelligence.

Good Stewardship is a Biblical Mandate

Related to the *imago-dei*, we see that God calls humans to have dominion over all creation under His divine leadership (Gen. 1:28). Ultimately, we recognize that everything we have belongs to the Lord (Psa. 24:1), and we have the opportunity (indeed, a mandate) to embrace a stewardship mindset, acknowledging our individual roles as managers and caretakers of his blessings. Part of this role involves careful stewardship of technology, which, of course, includes artificial intelligence.

The Church must play a crucial role in ensuring that AI is developed and used in ethically appropriate ways that honor God and promote human flourishing. Because we are image-bearers of the Lord and stewards of His creative work, we can once again ensure that AI never diminishes or disregards human worth but rather enhances and supports it.

To steward both creation and technology well, believers must engage in the discussion around AI. We must ask why, as we have already seen, prominent figures like Elon Musk and Stephen Hawking have sounded alarm bells. Why have prominent figures in the field, like Nick Bostrom, described the human flirtation with AI technology as "like children playing with a bomb"?[8] Why does he believe this is "quite possibly the most important and most daunting challenge humanity has ever faced?"[9] As God-ordained stewards of the earth, we must be sufficiently prepared to engage with and respond to these issues in a respectful, God-honoring, and Christlike manner. It is not enough to bury our heads in the sand, as tempting as it might seem. Change is coming, whether we accept it or not. The body of Christ must embrace their role as good stewards of the Earth before those changes are too detrimental to society.

We Are Called to Serve the Poor and Pursue Justice

Stewardship is an outworking of our role as image-bearers, and the outworking of stewardship is serving the poor and pursuing justice. The theological implications are vital for congregations seeking resilience concerning AI.

As we've seen, there is a genuine possibility that artificial intelligence may lead to a Singularity, particularly in the realm of economics. In *Surviving AI*, Calum Chace explains what might happen:

> An economic singularity might lead to an elite owning the means of production, and suppressing the rest of us in a dystopian technological authoritarian regime. Or it could lead to an economy of radical abundance, where nobody has to work for a living, and we are all free to have fun, stretch our minds, and develop our faculties to the full.[10]

It's worth noting that Chace is not articulating a fringe view but one shared by many others across various disciplines.[11] If these worst-case scenarios materialize, implementing artificial intelligence could potentially lead to unimaginable poverty. Were this to be the case, it's of paramount importance that the Church:

- Maintains a robust biblical theology of wealth and poverty
- Speaks up on behalf of the oppressed (with respect, integrity, and honor)
- Fulfills its duty to serve the poor
- Keeps an undistracted focus on the mission of the Church (Guideline 7).

By recognizing our responsibility as stewards of creation with a mandate to serve those in need, the Church will be well on the way to being prepared for the changes AI might bring.

We Must Maintain A Strong Theology of Work

Work is an integral part of God's original design for humanity. In the pre-Fall world of Genesis 2:15, God placed Adam in the Garden of Eden to "work it and take care of it." Clearly, there is something of intrinsic value about work. The Bible calls believers to work "with all their hearts, as working for the Lord and not for men" (Col. 3:23-24). We bring glory to the Lord through our labor. The very importance of a Sabbath rest implies the importance of work during the remainder of the week.

Entire books have been written about the importance and theology of work. For now, it's quite enough to recognize the importance of work to fulfill God's calling, serve others, provide for one another, and contribute to society. In the movie *Wall-E*, humans are aboard a "utopian" Starfleet where "robots do all the work and humans become decadent and lazy."[12] This type of vision is, in part, a backlash against work's increasingly all-consuming and "always-on" nature.

But there's something more at play here. In his book *Lost Connections*, Johann Hari undertook a lengthy exploration of the causes behind the depression epidemic in the Western world. His findings were interesting: work wasn't the enemy; the disconnection from *meaningful* work was.[13] Wallowing in gluttony and decadence isn't the answer because we're designed for purposeful work. What's important is the type of work that we do.

John Maynard Keynes—the economist who wrote to his wife about the potential he saw in a young Alan Turing—envisaged our near future in his 1930 essay *Economic Possibilities for Our Grandchildren*. He predicted that the "economic problem" (as he called it) would be solved, but that three-hour shifts or a fifteen-hour week "may put off the problem" of the "old Adam" urge in us to work so that we might "be contented."[14] Keynes was astute and eerily prophetic, recognizing a fundamental human need to work that God placed in the first humans. The fifteen-hour week may be imminent if AI ushers the world into an economic singularity. However, it seems that Keynes vastly underestimates this "old Adam" urge in humanity. Finding true purpose will take more than a few short hours of labor in the day. The Bible shows that work is a valuable, meaningful, and fulfilling part of life. Thus, to miss work and resign ourselves to lives of unadulterated, self-centered leisure time is to miss a fundamental part of God's design for us, which is no good thing. But these are not the musings of the Scriptures alone, though that would be enough. Studies are also beginning to bear this out:

The importance of having a job extends far beyond the salary attached to it. A large stream of research has shown that the non-monetary aspects of employment are also key drivers of people's well-being. Social status, social relations, daily structure, and goals all exert a strong influence on people's happiness.[15]

A healthy biblical theology of work will immunize us from the inherent emotional and spiritual dangers of a work-free economic singularity. Of course, we can (and should) utilize AI to be more effective in our work for the Lord, but we mustn't allow it to replace an essential aspect of our humanity. The more the global Church understands this fact, the more it will be able to weather the fast-approaching storms of change that rumble on the horizon.

We Are Called to Avoid Idolatry

In Exodus 20:3-5a, God makes it clear that we're to worship God alone; anything that holds a position higher than the Lord is idolatry (Psa. 115:4-8; Ezek. 14:3; Matt. 6:24; Acts 17:29). Given how our society is gripped by the digital world (social media, dating apps, pornography, etc.), it's easy to see how an increasingly artificially intelligent world could exacerbate the temptation to worship something other than God. We could veer into idolatry by placing excessive trust in man-made creations instead of the ultimate Creator, inadvertently elevating AI to an unhealthy position of ultimate authority in the process.

Such a reality sounds ridiculous, but it's not as far-fetched as we might think. Former Google engineer Anthony Levandowski committed perhaps the most egregious act of AI idolatry (or "AI-dolatry") in 2015 when he quite literally founded *The Way of the Future*, the first church of artificial intelligence. It closed its doors in 2021 but has experienced something of a resurgence in early 2024.[16] While this is a notable extreme, it's easy to see how AI-dolatry could sneak into our culture relatively undetected. As people in increasingly senior positions depend on this frontier technology to make or inform decisions, we may find ourselves dependent on (or shaped by) AI in all facets of our lives without even realizing it.

We can avoid the dangers of idolatry by keeping our eyes fixed on Jesus, the pioneer and perfecter of our faith (Heb. 12:2). We can continually remind ourselves of the importance of biblical wisdom, a powerful antidote to idolatry.

We Are Warned Against Pride

The Bible has much to say about the sin of pride. Consider the following passages:

- **Proverbs 16:18:** "Pride comes before destruction, and an arrogant spirit before a fall."
- **Proverbs 16:5:** "Everyone with a proud heart is detestable to the LORD; be assured, he will not go unpunished."
- **Proverbs 29:23:** "A person's pride will humble him, but a humble spirit will gain honor."

Micah 6:8 instructs us to *walk humbly* with our God. Jesus epitomized humility (Phil. 2:5-8), and God gives grace to the humble (Jam. 4:6). These are just a few passages that speak against the dangers of pride and the importance of humility (cf. Prov. 26:12; Jer. 9:23; Mark 7:20-23; Rom. 12:16; 1 Cor. 13:4; Gal. 6:3; Phil. 2:3; 1 Pet. 5:5).

As we just saw, a misplaced sense of pride in our abilities could lead to the misuse or elevation of artificial intelligence. Humility reveals the limitations of our creations and helps ensure their applications align with biblical principles.

The Bible teaches us that a healthy understanding of our place before God results in healthy humility. We're humble because we recognize our limitations and desperate need for grace. We're humble because we know God is the source of biblical wisdom, not human technology. We're humble because we know that God's ways and thoughts are higher than ours (Isa. 55:9). This truth remains regardless of whether humans can create a superintelligent artificial entity.

The Church can stay resilient to the coming technological, societal, and cultural effects of artificial intelligence by recognizing that its members are humans made in God's image, welcomed as God's children into his glorious household (1 Tim. 3:15; John 1:1-13; Rom. 8:16), called to be good stewards who serve the poor and pursue justice; those who recognize the value of work and avoid the sins of idolatry and pride. Such a perspective is a strong start and would likely have helped to stave off some of the negatives of Constantine's impact on the Church.

But that leads us to an important question: as leaders of any sort in the body of Christ, how might we best go about helping our congregation to become resilient believers? How can we help them ensure they build their houses on rock rather than sand?

Here are a few suggestions:

1. Help your church to see God in all His fullness, as much as possible.

Our perspective of God determines the direction of our lives. It's that simple. We will never be able to comprehend the majesty of the Lord. Even so, the more accurately we see him as he truly is, the more difficult it becomes to do anything but give our all to him.

Worship is the necessary response to a right view of God.

If we believe in a cheap, imitation, knock-off version of the One True God—a god of our limited design; less powerful, less gracious, less merciful, less holy, and less awesome and wonderful than the Lord God Almighty truly is—our faith will necessarily be found wanting. A small view of god breeds small faith. Unfortunately, this is too often the case. Instead of seeing a loving and all-surpassing King who is infinitely beyond human descriptors, we settle for an inaccurate, man-made image of Him, thus lowering our view of his power and our perspective of prayer. A distorted view of God is why so many people profess faith without ever really possessing it.

A proper perspective of God is the catalyst for worship, the antidote for idolatry, and the reason for iron-clad, immutable, and eternal security in an ever-changing world.

An accurate perspective of God leads to a rightful view of the world.

However, we must be specific here. A rightful view of the Lord is also intricately linked with the wonder of the gospel. Jesus's death, resurrection and ascension are essential in understanding God's grace, love, and mercy. It's freedom from the shackles of sin (1 Cor. 15:3), the gift of a new self (Eph. 4:17-24), and the open door for an indwelling of the Holy Spirit (Acts 1:8; 1 Cor. 3:16; Rom. 8:9)—all of which help us to see the wonder of God in higher resolution. Church leaders will go a long way to preparing their churches for the potential changes that AI will bring by simply encouraging brothers and sisters in Christ to elevate God to his rightful place as the undisputed King of all creation.

2. Help your church to grow in biblical literacy.

If our perspective of God determines the direction of our lives, the Bible is one of the primary means by which we can shape that perspective. For this reason, biblical literacy is critical. The great metanarrative of the Bible reveals God's nature, character, and attributes to us. As we gaze at Jesus, the Word who became flesh and dwelt among us (John 1:14), we're shown the Father (John 14:9). The entirety of the Scriptures points to God's majesty, plans, and purposes. The more we know the Bible and allow our hearts and minds to be shaped by it, the more our sense of awe and worship toward our Creator becomes inevitable.

Worship is a necessary response to a right view of God.

The problem of our time is that, wherever you look, biblical literacy and engagement are declining. A 2014 *Religious Landscape Study* conducted by the Pew Research Center found that fewer than 35% of adults read the Bible at least once a week.[17] Worse still, those figures appear to be decreasing. 2021-2022 saw an "unprecedented drop" in the number of US adults who read the Bible, with almost 26 million Americans reducing or stopping their interaction with Scripture, according to the American Bible Society's State of the Bible report.[18] At this critical juncture in history, church leaders must encourage believers to draw deep from the wells of Scripture. Aside from gaining a rightful perspective of God, there are several other significant reasons to strive for greater biblical literacy:

- To know objective truth in a subjective, post-truth world (Psa. 119:160; Isa. 40:8; John 17:17; Col. 2:8; 2 Tim. 3:16-17). The Bible is our lighthouse in a sea of misinformation.
- To strengthen our faith in trying times (Luke 8:11-15; Rom. 10:17; 15:4; 2 Tim. 3:15; Heb. 11;1).
- To provide us with moral and ethical guidance by offering principles, commandments, and teachings that instruct believers on living in a way that honors God, whatever the circumstance.

Because artificial intelligence is a wholly new field, the global Church is in somewhat uncharted territory, which is rare in a world where nothing is new under the sun (Ecc. 1:9). However, we can take confidence in that, while the field itself is unknown, the heart issues at the root of each problem are as

Guideline 2: Nurture Resilient Congregations

old as humanity itself. Those "old Adam urges" persist. Moving forward, we can best prepare for the coming changes that AI may bring by rooting ourselves firmly in God's Word.

3. Help your church strive towards biblical wisdom and healthy discernment.

With a rightful perspective of God and a deep understanding of the scriptures, we'll be well on the way toward exhibiting biblical wisdom—no matter the circumstance.

Because those sands are shifting faster than ever in our history, help establish strong biblical foundations your church community can lean on to make sense of what's happening; this will be essential as AI becomes an increasingly prominent part of everyday life. To build those foundations, you might consider encouraging intentional, thought-provoking discussions that aid believers in wrestling with the complexity of the sorts of topics we're addressing.

4. Help your church understand the potential changes AI may bring

This book was written with the express intention of helping address the potential changes and challenges on the horizon in light of artificial intelligence. Call it doom-mongering or due diligence, but either way, it's a clarion call to consider the bigger issues rearing their heads in our world. What are AI's theological, ethical, economic, societal, and cultural implications? What happens if we stumble into artificial general intelligence (AGI) or even the next phase, superintelligence? By understanding the gravity of the approaching change, we can ensure we're adequately equipped for the journey ahead.

How might you go about leading your church community to engage with AI? Here are a few suggestions:

1. Host a seminar or forum where you can discuss this topic in more depth.
2. Preach about the possible challenges and concerns around AI from the pulpit, as long as it's contextually and spiritually appropriate.
3. If you're uncomfortable speaking about the subject, invite a guest speaker to address the coming developments in AI. Don't bury your head in the sand!
4. Consider sharing this book with your church community or any others tackling AI from a biblical perspective. It doesn't have to be this one!

Weathering the Storm Together

Let's return to the banks of the Tiber. As Constantine crossed the Milvian Bridge, it's hard to imagine that any Roman believers—let alone believers around the known world—understood how profoundly the body of Christ would come to be affected by one victorious battle. It's often only in hindsight that we can look back on a seemingly innocuous moment and see its far-reaching consequences. Constantine's conversion changed the course of Christian history, just as so many other events have.

Here's why this matters. While the development of AI has trundled along in the background of the last century, our society has shifted. Will artificial intelligence foster a new cultural epoch that will shape our society for the next several decades? We can't say for sure, but we certainly can recognize that the potential is there. By fostering resilient congregations, embracing scriptural wisdom, and leading with discernment, church leaders can guide their communities to weather this storm and emerge from it more unified and steadfast in their pursuit of God. May we pray that the global Church stands firm on the rock and simultaneously sifts through these shifting sands to find the emerging gospel opportunities. To do that, we must prioritize relationship, community, and pastoral care and develop resilient congregations to weather the storms.

When these foundations are in place, we can look to Guideline 3: building adaptability into our church structures.

Reflection Questions for Guideline 2: Nurture Resilient Congregations

1. How might our understanding as humans made in God's image shape our approach to AI?

2. How does the concept of stewardship apply to our responsibility in developing and using artificial intelligence?

3. How does a biblical theology of work inform our understanding of the potential impact of AI on employment and human productivity?

4. What are the dangers of pride in the context of technological advancements like AI?

5. What practical steps can you help to help foster congregational resilience in your church community?

6. How does our perspective of God determine the direction of our life? How can the right perspective of God inform our approach to AI?

NOTES

[1] P. Schaff, "Article IV: Constantine the Great, and the Downfall of Paganism in the Roman Empire," *Bibliotecha Sacra* 20, no. 80 (1863), 778.

[2] Bruce Shelley and Marshall Shelley, "Church History in Plain Language, Fifth Edition" (Grand Rapids: HarperCollins Christian Publishing, 2021), 95.

[3] Justo L. González, *The Story of Christianity Volume One: The Early Church to the Reformation*, EPUB. (New York, NY: HarperCollins Publishers Inc., 2010), 208.

[4] Shelley and Shelley, "Church History in Plain Language, Fifth Edition", 100.

[5] González, *The Story of Christianity Volume One: The Early Church to the Reformation*, 233.

[6] Leithart, *Defending Constantine: The Twilight of an Empire and the Dawn of Christendom*.

[7] Shelley and Shelley, "Church History in Plain Language, Fifth Edition," 102.

[8] Adams, "Artificial Intelligence: 'We're like Children Playing with a Bomb' | Artificial Intelligence (AI) | The Guardian," last modified June 12, 2016, accessed May 22, 2023, https://www.theguardian.com/technology/2016/jun/12/nick-bostrom-artificial-intelligence-machine.

[9] Nick Bostrom, *Superintelligence* (Oxford: Oxford University Press, 2014), Kindle loc. 61 of 9985.

[10] Calum Chace, *Surviving AI*, Third Edition. (Three Cs, 2020), Kindle loc. 253 of 4658.

[11] Kai-Fu Lee and Chen Qiufan, *AI 2041* (New York: Currency, 2021); Michael E. Porter and James E. Heppelmann, "Why Every Organization Needs an Augmented Reality Strategy," in *HBR's 10 Must*

Reads On AI, Analytics, and the New Machine Age (Boston, MA: Harvard Business Review Press, 2019); Nick Bostrom, *Superintelligence* (Oxford: Oxford University Press, 2014); Derek C. Schuurman, "Artificial Intelligence: Discerning a Christian Response," *Perspectives on Science and Christian Faith* 71, no. 2 (2019); Annie Lowrey, "Before AI Takes Over, Make Plans to Give Everyone Money," *The Atlantic*, last modified May 17, 2023, accessed May 19, 2023, https://www.theatlantic.com/ideas/archive/2023/05/ai-job-losses-policy-support-universal-basic-income/674071/.

[12] Calum Chace, *Surviving AI*, Kindle loc. 2249 of 4658.

[13] Johann Hari, *Lost Connections: Uncovering the Real Causes of Depression - and the Unexpected Solutions* (New York, NY: Bloomsbury Publishing, 2018), 81.

[14] John Maynard Keynes, "Economic Possibilities for Our Grandchildren," in *Essays in Persuasion* (New York: W. W. Norton & Co., 1960), 369.

[15] Jan-Emmanuel De Neve and George Ward, "Does Work Make You Happy? Evidence from the World Happiness Report," *Harvard Business Review*, March 20, 2017, accessed May 8, 2023, https://hbr.org/2017/03/does-work-make-you-happy-evidence-from-the-world-happiness-report.

[16] Kirsten Korosec, "Anthony Levandowski Closes His Church of AI," *TechCrunch*, February 18, 2021, accessed May 11, 2023, https://techcrunch.com/2021/02/18/anthony-levandowski-closes-his-church-of-ai/.

[17] "Religious Landscape Study: Frequency of Reading Scripture," *Pew Research Center*, accessed February 13, 2024, https://www.pewresearch.org/religion/religious-landscape-study/.

[18] Jeffery Fulks, Randy Petersen, and John Farquhar Plake, "State of the Bible USA 2022" (The American Bible Society, 2022), x.

Guideline Three: Build Adaptability into Church Structures

Imagine millions of ordinary people plagued by a fear that technology is accelerating out of control. They worry that machines are coming to take away their jobs, erode their status, threaten their futures, and upend the order of their lives. Inequality is rampant, and power is wielded by those commanding wealth and new technologies. Every sign points to immense social and economic upheaval on the horizon. This could be today. It could also be two hundred years ago, in the early days of the Industrial Revolution, when the story of the rebellion against the use of those machines—and against the first tech titans—began.[1]

These are the poignant introductory words of Brian Merchant's book *Blood in the Machine: The Origins of the Rebellion Against Big Tech*. It's a fascinating and thought-provoking exploration of the Luddite uprising and the sorts of fears around industry-shaping technologies that parallel our cultural moment. The Luddites were a group of English textile workers who, in the early 19th Century, violently protested against the changes in their industry and the technological disruption wreaking havoc on the workforce.

It's understandable, really. The Industrial Revolution drastically changed our world and not always for the better—a fact Charles Dickens frequently and vividly depicted in classics like *Hard Times*, *Oliver Twist*, and *Bleak House*. The parallels with potential changes brought about by artificial intelligence are evident. There's a reason AI has been widely described as the "next Industrial Revolution."

The Church's response to artificial intelligence is critical. Is this the time to rebel like Luddites or adapt to the changes at hand?

I suggest both.

After pouring through tens of thousands of pages of research and trying to keep up with the latest news regarding AI—which, by the way, is like trying to swim up a waterfall—I'm increasingly convinced that the Body of Christ needs to

Guideline 3: Build Adaptability into Church Structures

both resist *and* embrace the coming technological revolution to varying degrees. I propose that the Church strive to be technological *semi-Luddites* concerning artificial intelligence.

This book is filled with technological optimism and an appeal to adaptation, sandwiched between some decidedly Luddite principles that eschew change for its own sake.

Consider the seven guidelines from this perspective:

1. Prioritize relationship, community, and pastoral care. **(Luddite)**
2. Nurture resilient congregations. **(Luddite)**
3. Build adaptability into church structures. **(Be Adaptable)**
4. Embrace positive technological developments. **(Be Adaptable)**
5. Stay informed in a rapidly changing environment. **(Neutral)**
6. Be proactive in praying for God-given wisdom. **(Luddite)**
7. Keep an undistracted focus on the mission of the Church. **(Luddite)**

Guidelines 1-2 and 6-7 call believers to rage against the dangers of the machine and stand firm in immutable, God-honoring biblical principles. They appeal to believers to resist the issues inherent in increasingly digitized pseudo-relationships and avoid letting a stodgy stew of AI-encouraged moral relativism overpower objective truth. A call to build on the rock, not the shifting sands of cultural, societal, and technological change (Matt. 7:24-27). To be intensely relational and resilient to the dangers of adverse change.

However, with those guidelines firmly established, Guidelines 3-4 encourage embracing helpful, purposeful, and sometimes inevitable change when beneficial to the gospel. We must resist throwing out the baby with the digital bathwater.

This chapter is a call to be *technological semi-Luddites*.

In this chapter, we'll discuss the need to build adaptability into our church structures to ensure ministry staff (and congregations) remain dynamic and responsive to the changes brought about by artificial intelligence. If we can succeed in doing this by the grace of God, we may witness incredible fruit for His Kingdom.

Understanding the Need for Adaptability

One of the common misconceptions in this conversation is the assumption that AI adaptability has one meaning only: "incorporating AI into ministry life." While this is undoubtedly part of the discussion, letting the conversation stop there is dangerously shortsighted. We need to think more broadly to serve our congregations and communities well.

It's not just our responsibility to adapt to technological changes as the Church. We must also recognize the impact these changes will have on our culture. In many ways, that's this book's thesis: AI's cultural impact will be more significant on the Church than its day-to-day implications. The

Guideline 3: Build Adaptability into Church Structures

landscape we minister in is changing, and the Church must adapt accordingly to be as effective as possible for the kingdom of God. We can minister well by looking beneath the surface issues and seeing how these broader changes affect our hearts. Our message does not change, but our practice might.

For this reason, it's useful for us to understand how our cultural landscape might change. We've already discussed the growing relational deficit in our society and AI's role as an accelerant. Let's add two other factors to the mix: the economy and education.

The Economy

As we've already seen, an AI-driven economic singularity could lead to "radical abundance where nobody has to work for a living" or an "elite owning the means of production and suppressing the rest of us in a dystopian technological authoritarian regime."[2] Which is the more likely? At this point, both scenarios are feasible. Time will tell.

It's not beyond the realms of possibility that we'll witness an explosion in economic abundance. From 1820 to 2010, there was a tenfold increase in global GDP per capita. However, AI brings humanity into a new territory that could bring similar growth in less time. Nick Bostrom explains what might happen in his book *Superintelligence:*

> Since GDP would soar following an intelligence explosion (because of massive amounts of new labor-substituting machines but also because of technological advances achieved by superintelligence, and, later,

acquisition of vast amounts of new land through space colonization), it follows that the total income from capital would increase enormously. If humans remain the owners of this capital, the total income received by the human population would grow astronomically, despite the fact that in this scenario humans would no longer receive any wage income. The human species as a whole could thus become rich beyond the dreams of Avarice."[3]

Most of the growth Bostrom refers to relates in some form to increased productivity. In 2023, Accenture studied AI's impact on the workplace and reached some stunning conclusions. Paul Daugherty, the company's Group Chief Executive and Chief Technology Officer who helped author the study, estimated that soon, as many as 40% of *all* working hours could be significantly enhanced or supported by large language models like ChatGPT.[4] Such predictions aren't challenging to find support for elsewhere, underscoring the profound impact many anticipate artificial intelligence will have on the workplace. However, the potential benefits of AI extend beyond efficiency alone. As Kai-Fu Lee and Chen Qiufan explain in their book *AI-2041*, the proliferation of AI-enhanced technology in various sectors—including manufacturing, autonomous vehicles, and unmanned aerial vehicles (drones)—looks to revolutionize many traditional job roles. Indeed, this sort of technological change may be able to "take over routine tasks and liberate us to do more stimulating or challenging jobs."[5] In this sense, the shifting

Guideline 3: Build Adaptability into Church Structures

sands of industry could allow humans to unleash greater creativity and innovation, removing some mundane tasks and potentially elevating the quality of one's work life.

In turn, increased productivity could radically lower transport and labor costs (which, in turn, would lower the general cost of goods for the consumer), as AI-enhanced robotics don't require payment and can work twenty-four hours a day, seven days a week. In other words, it's possible that the general cost of goods rapidly decreases while our income stays the same.

That's the best-case scenario.

However, widespread use of AI technology could potentially cause "unprecedented job displacement . . . that will hit blue- and white-collar workers alike."[6] Some project that almost half of these jobs are at risk of being replaced by AI in certain nations, causing the gap between rich and poor to increase and, in turn, bringing about vastly more social problems and civil unrest.[7] However, governments could conceivably redistribute the enormous economic surplus generated by this technology through support schemes or a version of the universal basic income (UBI).[8] In such a scenario, it's not beyond the realms of possibility that poverty is eradicated and work becomes optional for many. While alleviating poverty would, of course, be a cause for celebration, other challenges come with initiatives like UBI.

On the other hand, a potential decline in the availability of jobs may radically increase competition and thus drive down wages.[9] Such an occurrence is problematic when there is already concern about the growing disparity between wages and the cost of living. However, as the global economy continues to consolidate around digital superpowers such as Alphabet, Amazon, Apple, Facebook, Microsoft, and Alibaba, this power balance grows more disparate.[10] Marco Iansiti and Karim Lakhani note that while these organizations create value for their users, "these companies are also capturing a disproportionate and expanding share of the value, and that's shaping our collective economy futures." It's a concerning state of affairs. Iansiti and Lakhani conclude, "If current trends continue, the hub economy will spread across more industries, further concentrating data, value, and power in the hands of a small number of firms employing a tiny fraction of the workforce."[11] Once again, AI will only make this reality more acute.

Education

Artificial intelligence may be both a help and a hindrance to education. In some ways, providing highly competent AI tutors at negligible cost may significantly support the educational process.[12] My preschool-aged children will grow up with the world's information at their fingertips—a reality that is both positive and negative. AI systems can guide them through the learning process with relative ease, quickly explaining concepts in more straightforward or simply different ways depending on their learning styles.

As someone (only just) old enough to have missed the YouTube boom and the vast ocean of free tutorials on the platform during my school years, I enormously struggled when we had a less-than-stellar teacher or if I didn't understand the textbook. There were no other avenues of learning except for hiring a private tutor, which we couldn't afford. Today, and even more so with artificial intelligence, future generations are no longer dependent on a single, financially prohibitive educational path, which, intellectually speaking, can be a massive blessing for students today.

Einstein is usually attributed with the saying, "Everyone is a genius. But if you judge a fish by its ability to climb a tree, it will live its whole life believing that it is stupid." Although Einstein never *actually* said this, the sentiment is nevertheless true. AI can help students excel by leveraging personalized learning paths tailored to their strengths, interests, and learning styles. The benefit to society could be vast.

However, as we saw in Guideline 1, AI can only get you so far. Education is more than *just* information transfer. Kai-Fu Lee and Chen Qiufan predict that this is why traditional human teachers will remain extremely valuable:

> Teachers will play two important roles: First, they will be human mentors and connectors for the students. Human teachers will be the driving force behind stimulating the students' critical thinking, creativity, empathy, and teamwork. And the teacher will be a clarifier when a student is confused, a confronter when the student is complacent, and a comforter when the student is frustrated. In other words, teachers can focus less on the rote aspects of imparting knowledge and more on building emotional intelligence, creativity, character, values, and resilience in students.[13]

Once again, we see the sheer potency and importance of human connection. Increasing the quality of holistic education while simultaneously lowering costs would be a near-miraculous feat, but as with most things, it's not quite as simple as it might seem. There are considerable hurdles

Further integrating AI into distractive forces such as social media, which have already been shown to have adverse effects on adolescents, could be disastrous in the field of education.[14] Advanced AI systems are consummate weapons of mass *distraction* that can "track an individual's online reading habits, preferences, and likely state of knowledge, [and] tailor specific messages to maximize impact on that individual while minimizing the risk that the information will be disbelieved."[15] The level of attention-sucking noise that students must contend with today is mind-boggling; AI—the Great Exacerbater—can improve the potency of the distraction. Without ethical oversight, we may experience torrents of disinformation and artificial realities, with some experts predicting that as much as 90% of online content "may be synthetically generated by 2026."[16] Such concerns are the source of apprehension around an "information apocalypse," where disinformation and deepfake technology are so ubiquitous that it becomes increasingly difficult to separate fact from fiction.

Additionally, with artificial intelligence comes the vast potential for plagiarism. How do educators combat the possibility that students can bypass the learning process altogether? I serve as an academic advisor at a Bible college here in Canada. As we've wrestled with this issue, I've found the following questions and positions helpful:

First, *trying to run a plagiarism check for AI-written content seems like a fool's errand.* Ultimately, it is far too easy for a student to ask an LLM like ChatGPT or Google Gemini to write something for them and disguise it in their own words. If executed with any modicum of skill, the line between artificially and organically written becomes so blurry that it's almost impossible to discern one from the other. If we're too overzealous, we risk starting a witch hunt and burning innocents at the stake in the process. If the students contest or appeal the decision, how can we prove beyond reasonable doubt that the AI checker is correct, especially when it only gives a percentage probability?

Second, *should* we limit students from using AI? If so, to what extent? How would this be different from banning students from using traditional search engines like Google or calculators for their mathematical exercises? Again, this is a gray area. As we'll see in the next chapter, LLMs—like search engines and calculators—can be valuable tools in their proper context, as long as the student is developing the appropriate skills and knowledge base required to be a benefit to society.

Third, might we see a rise in exam-based competency tests rather than long-form assignments to avoid plagiarism? At present, students would struggle to sneak an AI-driven device into an examination room, so they'd have to depend on their own abilities. While this allows faculty to guarantee a certain level of competence in a student, to what extent is rote memory helpful in a world where AI makes knowledge instantaneous and interactive? Would we develop redundant competence by hiding it from AI's supplemental capabilities?

Given the post-truth, highly individualistic nature of the world we inhabit, it could potentially be more helpful to develop foundational skills in logical reasoning and emotional intelligence, and allow students to pursue information using all the tools available, as long as the student maintains a clear standard of academic rigor and integrity to the best of their ability. But this is highly subjective and, in many cases, impossible to quantify.

One approach I've taken with my undergraduate students is simply saying, yes, you *can* choose to let AI write your papers for you in secret, and it's likely that I won't be able to tell. But:

1. If I *can* tell, that's a big problem for you and your possible future at the school, as any plagiarism would be.
2. You are wasting the time and money you've invested in building a skill set that will make you valuable to the world. The piece of paper you get for your degree may look nice and might open a door or two for you, but it's largely worthless if you don't have the appropriate knowledge and abilities to accompany it.
3. You are taking a considerable risk, as you'll eventually get found out in the real world. The gaps in your understanding where you let AI do all the heavy lifting will not help you as you prepare for the work you are hoping to do. You are jeopardizing your chances of long-term employability when you *could* instead make the

most of your studies to be equipped for the work that awaits.
4. You're making a significant statement about your character and integrity here. In the secular world, that's a problem, but as believers, that is *devastating*.

Such a response is clearly not foolproof by any means, but it's been helpful in my context so far. However it might look, we can be confident that education will significantly change in the next decade or two.

Where does this leave us? So far, we've seen profound cultural changes concerning sexuality, individualism, political divides, the growing digitization of relationships, and the mental health crises that have accompanied them. We've built a case for resilient congregations in this changing world and recognized that two of the core pillars of our society—economics and education—could be utterly transformed in the coming years. We're undergoing an unfathomably widespread change. The world as we know it is shifting, but:

On Christ the solid Rock, I stand;
  All other ground is sinking sand,
    All other ground is sinking stand.

It's doubtful that the Church will remain untouched by today's profound cultural, societal, economic, and technological changes. As AI technologies increase, they will inevitably change communication, community engagement, and possibly even spiritual practices, although this is shaky ground that warrants significant conversation. However, before we get there, we must understand the need for adaptability within our ministry contexts. Churches cannot remain static in this evolving landscape; they must be agile and adaptable to minister effectively to their communities. Our foundations will never change—on Christ the solid Rock we stand—but perhaps as the gathered Body of Christ, we need to make some renovations to our houses (without changing the foundations) in order to better connect with and serve our changing environment. How might we go about doing this?

Regularly Assess the Effectiveness of Your Church's Practices

We Protestants are quick to challenge the traditionalism of the Catholic church but often hypocritically embrace watered-down or low-key versions of it in our settings. It's tempting to make golden calves or sacred cows out of perfectly fine but non-essential elements of ministry. If you don't believe me, consider the following questions as a taster of our traditionalism:

- Why is it expected that "good" churches serve coffee at a worship gathering?
- Why is it standard practice (in evangelical circles, at least) for a sermon to be between twenty and forty minutes? When was the last time a sermon went on late into the night, like Paul in Acts 20, and the ushers had to close the windows to stop a modern-day Eutychus falling out?
- Why is "contemporary worship" music a *genre* that the musically inclined can recognize without hearing a

single word sung? As a former worship pastor, I wonder why we have a persistent (false) belief that the Holy Spirit only wants to move when "ambient pads" are lingering in the background or if there is enough reverb and delay on the electric guitar signal.

- Why have we persisted in passing around offering baskets in an almost entirely cashless society?
- Why do we refer to people as "Pastor [name]" but not "Elder [name]," "Teacher [name]" (or pastor-teacher, depending on your preference), or "Evangelist [name]"?
- Why do churches discuss being "free" in worship yet follow the same loose liturgies each week? You know the one: Sung worship, notices, sermon, response (or some minor alteration of it—occasionally with communion).

I'm sure you could think of at least a dozen or so other examples that speak to the implicit desire for tradition in our worship. Let me be clear: nothing outlined above is inherently wrong, but these practices gain a distinctly golden sheen and bovine silhouette when we make them immutable *expectations*. Perhaps we don't even realize we're doing it. To respond to our changing world in a God-honoring way, we must start by recognizing the preference in our praxis.

Adaptability begins with a regular assessment of church processes and structures. Wise churches will continuously evaluate how they conduct their ministries, deliver services, and engage with communities. This evaluation should consider the changing cultural context, be prepared to assess the potential impact of AI technologies and seek healthy ways to integrate them to benefit the kingdom of God. Here are some potentially helpful diagnostic questions:

- Is this ministry area or expression of church life a biblical imperative?
  Example: Communion: Absolutely. Coffee before the service: not so much. It's just nice.

- Are we stuck in our ways or genuinely open to God-honoring change for the sake of the gospel (1 Cor. 9:19-23)? Or, to put it another way, am I guilty of using the phrase "that's just how we do it here" without actually considering if there's a biblical foundation that underpins it or a potentially more effective way to achieve the desired outcome?
  Example: The structure of Sunday gatherings, small groups, staffing practices, etc.

- Does our staffing structure best serve our congregation and surrounding community? If not, are we willing to make difficult calls to change it?
  Example: If relational issues become more prominent in our societies, could AI's increased productivity and efficiency mean hiring fewer administrative staff and more pastors to meet that need?

- Are there unhelpful sacred cows in our thinking or practice?
  Example: AI is "from the devil," or "technology always makes ministry more effective." Neither statement is helpful.

Guideline 3: Build Adaptability into Church Structures

- Where are the fresh gospel opportunities in this changing world, and are we well-equipped to respond to them?
  Example: Relational evangelism may be more effective than large outreach and entertainment events in a world starved of meaningful social connections where on-demand entertainment is available at any moment.

Considerations for Churches in a World of AI

Let's start to pull these various threads together.

Irrespective of your position on AI inside the church, you cannot escape the fact that AI will dramatically affect the world around it. To adapt to the changing needs of society, we'd be wise to build a culture of adaptability into church structures. Leaders can begin preparing ministries for AI's cultural, technological, and economic impact so they can readily and quickly respond to gospel opportunities as they arise. Or, put another way, the church can appropriately contextualize its message to the community it serves. Timothy Keller explains contextualization in the following helpful way:

> Contextualization is not — as is often argued — "giving people what they want to hear." Rather, it is giving people the Bible's answers, which they may not at all want to hear, to questions about life that people in their particular time and place are asking, in language and forms they can comprehend, and through appeals and arguments with

force they can feel, even if they reject.[17]

Contextualization is appropriate in a changing world. Proactive rather than reactive churches are better prepared to be effective in their mission.
Tear down those sacred cows if you need to.
Soften those Luddite hearts if you have to.

Artificial intelligence could be both a blessing and a curse inside the church. Here are a few examples:
By adopting AI tools for scheduling, resource management, and even financial tracking, churches may be able to divert administrative costs toward pastoral care. Adapting to elevate meaningful connections may be extremely wise in a world facing a radical relational deficit. Are we laying the groundwork for these positive changes?
Conversely, it's only a matter of time—mark my words—before a megachurch pastor of some form creates an artificial version of themselves to "pastor" their burgeoning flock on their behalf.

The very thought makes me shudder.

Similarly, as AI drastically improves education, could traditional seminary education be rendered obsolete? The depressing reality of cost-prohibitive barriers to ministry in some circles could be significantly reduced or even eliminated, opening the floodgates for genuinely "called" but financially limited ministers of the gospel to enter the pastorate. It's possible that biblical literacy across the board could increase, and church leaders could give more attention to character

Guideline 3: Build Adaptability into Church Structures

rather than competency. Are we laying the groundwork for these positive changes in our churches?

On the other hand, the opposite could also be true. Future ministers could potentially depend on AI to write their papers for them, study for them, and give them the appearance of competency without any of the character. In a Western society with a widespread shortage of pastors, this could be devastating for the Church.

More broadly, a new frontier of evangelism may open. gospel opportunities may skyrocket as we encourage a culture of adaptive innovation, creative thinking, experimentation, and a willingness to try new approaches and explore the opportunities that arise from AI. By positioning the church to respond effectively to the changing societal landscape, we may see great fruit for God's kingdom. AI-enhanced biblical translation may utterly transform our world. Are we laying the groundwork for these positive changes in our churches?

However, once again, there are challenges here. There are risks in allowing machines to translate the inspired Word of God. If it's biased or faulty, the consequences could be dire. But challenges require prudence, not total prohibitions.

A critical aspect of adaptability is ensuring that church staff and volunteers are trained and equipped at least to understand (if not handle) new technologies and methodologies. Regular training sessions, workshops, and resources on AI and digital tools will empower them to serve effectively in a rapidly changing environment.

It's worth briefly commenting on the economic changes that may take place in our time. As tempting as it is to imagine a society "rich beyond the dreams of Avarice," where everyone's basic needs are met, it's unlikely that poverty will be eradicated. Jesus told us we will always have the poor with us (Matt. 26:11; Mark 14:7; John 12:8), so while our overall economic situation may improve, alleviating poverty in our time is most likely an unfortunate impossibility.

Finally, preparing the congregation for change is vital in building adaptability. Church leaders should communicate the benefits and challenges of integrating AI into church life, set realistic expectations, and foster an open-minded culture among the congregation. However, this can only come if an appropriately semi-Luddite congregational resilience looks cautiously toward the more dangerous aspects of AI.

Practical Steps for Becoming Adaptable Churches

Hopefully, you're convinced of the need to be technological semi-Luddites who adapt to the changing technology and, more importantly, pivot with the changing culture in which we live to be maximally effective for God's glory. Here are some practical steps for becoming churches that can adapt to the coming changes that artificial intelligence will bring about:

1. **Look for any unhealthy sacred cows in your church practices, and help the church recognize them for what they are.** By doing this, you are preparing the church to focus on what matters and to release redundant practices should the need arise.

2. **Foster a healthy sentiment toward change while remaining clear on what is unchangeable.** John Kotter's *8 Steps for Leading Change* is invaluable here:

Guideline 3: Build Adaptability into Church Structures

I. Create a Sense of Urgency
II. Build a Guiding Coalition
III. Form a Strategic Vision
IV. Enlist a Volunteer Army
V. Enable Action by Removing Barriers
VI. Generate Short-Term Wins
VII. Sustain Acceleration
VIII. Institute Change[18]

Now is a perfect time to create a sense of urgency (I) and surround yourself with a guiding coalition to help instigate future change (II). Lay the foundations now. Be proactive, not reactive. Take some time to assess the church's unchangeable focuses (e.g., preaching the gospel, meaningful connection, etc.).

3. **Encourage the church (especially leaders) to be well-informed regarding culture and artificial intelligence.** It's tempting to keep our heads in the sand and hide from these encroaching changes. However, doing so is unhelpful as it potentially lessens our effectiveness for the gospel and minimizes our opportunity to proactively meet our communities' needs. Whether through seminars, videos, or even books like this, encourage the church to engage with culture, not to shy away from it.

4. **If necessary, be prepared to restructure the church now.** Noah would have been in trouble if he ignored the Lord and started building the Ark when it began to rain. The same applies to the wise man who built his house

on the rock. Perhaps your church community needs to make fundamental structural changes to weather the coming AI storm and resulting cultural shifts. Now is the time to do it. For example, can you provide the pastoral care you will inevitably need? Do you have the teams and processes in place to foster resilient congregations? Can someone directly support your congregation as these cultural changes take hold, or use the opportunities they provide? There are *many* questions here, and most are specific to your setting.

Navigating the Challenges of Change

Change is rarely comfortable for everyone, and we often meet it with resistance. Transitioning to new ways of operating can be challenging. Church leaders must navigate these situations with sensitivity and wisdom, providing clear communication, support, and guidance.

Be a technological semi-Luddite who prepares your church family for the inevitable changes that are on the way.

Building adaptability into church structures is critical for church leaders in the AI era. It's not just about keeping pace with technology; it's about faithfully stewarding the call of the Great Commission in an ever-changing world. By staying informed, being open to change, and equipping congregations to navigate the challenges of this new landscape, church leaders can play their small part in ensuring their ministries remain effective and impactful in an ever-evolving world while all the while remembering that God is ultimately the one who brings the growth.

Reflection Questions for Guideline 3: Build Adaptability into Church Structures

1. What specific "sacred cows" might your church need to re-evaluate in light of our changing world?

2. We discussed being "technological semi-Luddites." In general, are you more prone to embracing or rejecting technological advances? Have you considered how this might be helpful and unhelpful, depending on the situation?

3. Do you think church staffing practices might change in light of artificial intelligence? If so, how? If not, why?

4. How can churches balance adaptability with maintaining their core values and identity?

5. Following John Kotter's *8 Steps for Leading Change*, how might church leaders effectively create a sense of urgency and build a guiding coalition regarding artificial intelligence?

6. How can individual believers support their churches in becoming more adaptable and responsive to change while maintaining resilient congregations?

NOTES

[1] Brian Merchant, *Blood in the Machine* (New York: Little, Brown and Company), 2023), 22.

[2] Chace, *Surviving AI*, Kindle loc. 253 of 4658.

[3] Bostrom, *Superintelligence,* Kindle loc. 4162 of 9985.

[4] Paul Daugherty, "A.I. Will Potentially Impact 40% of Your Working Hours, According to Accenture," *Fortune*, last modified 2023, accessed July 21, 2023, https://fortune.com/2023/05/11/ai-impact-work-hours-accenture-careers-tech-paul-daugherty/

[5] Kai-Fu Lee and Chen Qiufan, AI 2041 (New York: Currency, 2021), Kindle loc. 132 of 7291

[6] Ibid., Kindle loc. 5743 of 7291.

[7] Carl Benedikt Frey and Michael A. Osborne, "The Future of Employment: How Susceptible Are Jobs to Computerisation?," *Technological Forecasting and Social Change* 114 (2017): 254–280; John C., *2084: Artificial Intelligence and the Future of Humanity* (Grand Rapids, MI: Zondervan Reflective, 2020), 13.

[8] Annie Lowrey, "Before AI Takes Over, Make Plans to Give Everyone Money," *The Atlantic*, last modified May 17, 2023, accessed May 19, 2023, https://www.theatlantic.com/ideas/archive/2023/05/ai-job-losses-policy-support-universal-basic-income/674071/.

[9] Carl Benedikt Frey and Michael A. Osborne, "The Future of Employment: How Susceptible Are Jobs to Computerisation?," *Technological Forecasting and Social Change* 114 (2017): 254–280.

[10] Marco Iansiti and Karim R. Lakhani, "Managing Our Hub Economy," in *HBR's 10 Must Reads On AI, Analytics, and the New Machine Age* (Boston, MA: Harvard Business Review Press, 2019), 123.

[11] Ibid.

[12] Russell, *Human Compatible: Artificial Intelligence and the Problem of Control*, Kindle loc. 1827 of 7202.

[13] Lee and Qiufan, *AI 2041*, Kindle loc. 2122 of 7291.

[14] Jean M. Twenge, "Have Smartphones Destroyed a Generation?," *The Atlantic*, last modified September 2017, accessed May 30, 2022, https://www.theatlantic.com/magazine/archive/2017/09/has-the-smartphone-destroyed-a-generation/534198/;

Jonathan Haidt Schmidt Eric, "AI Is About to Make Social Media (Much) More Toxic," *The Atlantic*, last modified May 5, 2023, accessed July 21, 2023, https://www.theatlantic.com/technology/archive/2023/05/generative-ai-social-media-integration-dangers-disinformation-addiction/673940/.

[15] Russell, *Human Compatible: Artificial Intelligence and the Problem of Control*, Kindle Loc. 1893 of 7202.

[16] Europol Innovations Lab, *Facing Reality? Law Enforcement and the Challenge of Deepfakes* (Luxembourg: Publications Office of the European Union, 2022).

[17] Timothy Keller, *Center Church* (Grand Rapids, MI: Zondervan, 2012), Kindle loc. 2249 of 12795.

[18] Alex Bedard, "The 8-Step Process for Leading Change | Dr. John Kotter," *Kotter International Inc*, n.d., accessed February 10, 2024, https://www.kotterinc.com/methodology/8-steps/.

Guideline Four: Embrace Positive Change

The year is roughly 1013. A young traveler journeys through picturesque Italian countryside and enjoys the warm breeze brushing his face. In truth, he's far more interested in his horse's percussive hoofing of the ground, noting how it neatly accentuates the slow trundle of the carriage he's bumping along on. His ears are well-trained for such rhythms.

As he pulls on the reins, the rider slows to the magnificent view of Pomposa Abbey. It's an imposing place of worship and residence for the Benedictine monks he would live with for the next decade. While the relaxing sounds of the horse and cart have faded, there's no space for silence. A muffled but unmistakable sound seeps through the Abbey's windows. It's a chorus of future comrades, a beautiful, almost divine melody of monks singing in perfect unison. The traveler, who would one day be known by the moniker Guido D'Arezzo, closes his eyes and breathes in this moment before letting out a delighted sigh. This exquisite choir was all the confirmation he needed. He was home.

Guido's time at Pomposa Abbey would go on to shape the world. A prodigious musical talent, it was within the hallowed halls of Pomposa that he would invent—or at the very least, develop—the first system for transcribing music, a precursor to the modern sheet music that has dominated musical history for centuries. Before Guido, one would teach music by rote, which had considerable limitations. It was time-consuming and highly restricted by fallible and insubstantial memories.

With transcribed music, musicians could perform more intricate compositions in a fraction of the time. The beautiful choral music Guido may have heard on his arrival was merely the tip of the iceberg, a taster of the dazzling harmonies his invention would one day inspire. Guido's system gained rapid popularity in the area as people began to recognize the significance of the young monk's achievement. But while this technological achievement left most of the province awash with enthusiasm, some of Guido's colleagues—and unfortunately, even the Abbott—grew skeptical, critical, and jealous. They were uncomfortable with the new system and didn't hesitate to inform its inventor of their feelings. Around a decade after arriving at Pomposa, they forced Guido to leave. He headed for Arezzo, where he would—quite literally—make his name.

The rest, as they say, is history.

Guideline 4: Embrace Positive Change

Guido D'Arezzo's notation system laid the foundations for much of the music that would follow and, as a result, profoundly impacted the Church he had devoted his life to serving.

> Thanks to Guido, we have Bach's *St. Matthew Passion*.
> Thanks to Guido, we have Handel's *Messiah*.
> Thanks to Guido, we have Newton's *Amazing Grace*.
> Thanks to Guido, we have Redman's *10,000 Reasons*.
> Thanks to Guido, we have Pinkfong's *Baby Shark*.

Ok. So it's not all good news.

Guido's musical notation was an invention that proved to be a decisive moment in history and culture. It also serves as a valuable reminder that not all technological advances are negative. Some technological developments can be extraordinarily beneficial to the Church.

As 21st Century believers wrestle with the coming changes that artificial intelligence will inevitably bring, we have three choices:

1. We can act like Guido D'Arezzo's fellow monks, either burying our heads in the sand or defaulting to criticism.
2. We can run like banshees toward every technological development without stopping to see whether it's *actually* beneficial or not.
3. We can step forward into the developments of our time like technological semi-Luddites, those who separate the wheat from the chaff, embrace the former, and ditch the latter.

In the previous chapter, I argued for the third position: that we should strive to be a church of semi-Luddites. In the following pages, I hope to persuade you that rather than simply accepting positive developments in artificial intelligence and technology in general, we should actively *encourage* them. The argument is simple:

- **Premise 1:** History shows us that some technological developments have greatly benefited the Church.
- **Premise 2:** There are myriad ways that artificial intelligence *could* conceivably benefit the Church.
- **Conclusion:** Therefore, the Church should actively embrace and encourage the appropriate adoption of artificial intelligence where the technology can further its mission and effectiveness in the modern world while being aware of potential concerns.

Suspend your disbelief for a moment. Soften those Luddite hearts if you have to. How we respond to the coming changes could define a generation of ministry.

How Tech Has Changed the Church

You might feel compelled to skip this section if you're an unabashed techno-optimist. But if you're on the fence or perhaps seething at the thought of using artificial intelligence anywhere near the body of Christ, consider three ways technology has greatly helped the global Church over the centuries.

Guideline 4: Embrace Positive Change

1. The Printing Press

In 1436, Johannes Gutenberg invented the printing press, changing the world forever. It used movable type, which meant that books could be created significantly faster, cheaper, and more accurately than ever before. Supposedly, the first book printed in Europe was the Latin Vulgate in the 1450s—also known as the "Gutenberg Bible"—although this may be apocryphal.[1] Whatever the case, the printing press was a technological marvel that resulted in the democratization of knowledge and the beginnings of the Protestant Reformation.

In other words, it was a big deal for the Church.

Roughly two hundred years after Gutenberg's printing press, Giovanni Andrea Bussi noted the drastic changes it had brought about in a letter to Pope Paul II: ". . .God gave Christendom a gift which enables even the pauper to acquire books. Prices of books have decreased by eighty percent."[2]

An *eighty* percent decrease in book costs! Coupled with the simultaneous developments in Bible translations during the same period, believers of all walks of life could finally afford to purchase and study the Word of God for themselves. There aren't many today who would view the invention of the printing press as anything other than a landmark achievement that has utterly and positively transformed our world.

But at the time, not everyone thought it was a good thing.

In the open-air pulpit of Old Saint Paul's Cathedral in London, England, the Vicar of Croydon supposedly proclaimed to his congregation, "either we must root out printing, or it will root us out."[3] He saw it as a threat to the authority of the Church and its ability to disseminate prescribed doctrine. In 1563, John Foxe (famous for his *Book of Martyrs*) also recognized the significance of the change. In light of the printing press, he wrote,

> . . .hereby tongues are known, knowledge groweth, judgment increaseth, books are dispersed, the Scripture is seen, the doctors be read, stories be opened, times compared, truth discerned, falsehood detected, and with finger pointed, and all, as I said, through the benefit of printing. . . either the pope must abolish printing, or he must seek a new world to reign over; for else, as this world standeth, printing doubtless will abolish him.[4]

The papal office never found a "new world to reign over" or had any success in abolishing printing. However, the printing press helped spark a Reformation that shook the world to its core. This almost miraculous invention brought incredible technological development. Indeed, we have only begun to entertain ideas of a "paperless" digital world in the last several decades, nearly *eight hundred* years after the invention of the printing press. But it also brought discontent and discomfort for those quite satisfied with the status quo. Change is hard when we're not the ones initiating it.

2. Radio

It's easy for us to forget how profoundly radio changed the world. After several decades of developments, the 1920s ushered in the birth of commercial radio and, in so doing, brought about an entirely new form of media: the almost magical ability to hear voices almost instantly from hundreds, if not thousands, of miles away. In a fascinating article for Christianity Today, Mark Rogers detailed how Paul Rader pioneered the technology for gospel purposes, recognizing that it could "push out the walls of the biggest church and reach the unsaved man."[5] Radar was followed by early techno-optimists Fulton J. Sheen and Walter A. Maier, who, through the medium, "fundamentally reshaped what it meant to be Lutheran, Catholic, evangelical, and Christian in America."[6] By the 1940s, millions would hear the Good News of Jesus every week from within the confines of their homes via the radio. A humbled Sheen noted how radio had made it possible to "address more souls in the space of thirty minutes than St. Paul did in all his missionary journeys."[7]

Today, in a world of video calls and on-demand streaming, it's easy to see radio as an archaic and dated form of technology. But in truth, it changed the face of ministry forever. Radio was a transformative tool for evangelism, Christian preaching, and general education in remote or inaccessible areas.

However, once again, not everyone supported the changes that were taking place at the time. There were concerns that radio would irrevocably damage the world. Some believers, recognizing that the devil was the prince of the power of the air (Eph. 2:2), felt the airwaves were his domain and not to be tampered with. As with the printing press, those rumbles of discontent lingered. Now, those fears have been all but assuaged. In truth, most evangelicals embraced radio reasonably quickly, and it transformed the world's communicative abilities as a result.

3. Audiovisual Technology

In the 1990s, the relationship between traditional musical notation and the Church—birthed out of Guido D'Arezzo's work all those centuries earlier—endured a significant blow. In many evangelical churches, believers threw out hymnals en masse in favor of a little glowing box called an overhead projector. For generations too young to remember them, an overhead projector worked by shining light through a transparent sheet and projecting whatever was printed (or hand-written) on them to a screen or wall. It was another revolution, changing how believers worshiped together. No longer did church-goers have to thumb through the pages in frantic search of the prescribed hymn. Lyrics were easier than ever to follow, and those with fading eyesight benefitted from a much larger font. The projected image could be enormous.

All of this meant that congregants could, in theory, give greater attention to undistracted worship—the very thing they had joined with their fellow believers to do. Churches operating on a shoestring budget no longer had to pay for dozens—if not hundreds—of expensive hymnals, meaning those finances could be better spent elsewhere. The hymnal's repertoire was no longer restrictive for worship leaders (though some may argue that this was detrimental). Churches could project Biblical passages onto a screen for those new to

Guideline 4: Embrace Positive Change

the faith or unfamiliar with God's Word. It was a significant change for the Church and an obvious precursor to how many churches use technology in worship today. But you're probably getting the idea by now.

It wasn't for everyone.

Some people fiercely attacked this technological change. One complaint from a 1999 magazine article took the change quite poorly: "The joy of singing worshipful songs is replaced by frustration in trying to learn or recall the tune."[8] Some felt that the lack of written traditional sheet music stifled praises and that Guido's good work had been gutted.

Nowadays, digital projection has almost entirely replaced its analog predecessor, and those earlier concerns have all but evaporated into the past. Though not unheard of, it is certainly the exception, rather than the norm, for evangelical churches to use hymnals rather than some sort of presentation software.

A Familiar Response to Technology

These monumental inventions point us to a single truth. Did you catch the noticeable parallels with the development of the printing press, radio ministry, and developments in audiovisual technology?

It's improbable that anyone today would question how at least *the majority* of these technological changes have revolutionized our worship. Yet, at the time, there was significant pushback. There are a plethora of other technological developments that we could also explore, where the initial resistance was the same: musical recording, the internet, television, live streaming, and mobile apps, to name a few. In many ways, these changes were controversial in their time but have become widely accepted parts of church life and practice today.

Here's the point: it's sometimes appropriate to have concerns over technological developments. For this reason, we must have strong foundations in place. But it's also important to recognize that sometimes our fears are born out of little more than an uncomfortable relationship with the unknown. Put another way, maybe we're just change-averse for its own sake, and that's not such a good thing. Grab that pair of rose-tinted spectacles. Get ready for a healthy dose of optimism (with appropriate balance) in the following pages.

How AI Might Change the Church

In the last chapter, we explored how AI might impact the church, exploring the need for adaptability in our churches. But it's worth delving a little deeper. It's one thing to be *adaptable* to technological developments; it's another to *embrace* them. So, how might artificial intelligence change the Church for the better?

1. AI for Bible Translation

According to Wycliffe Global Alliance's *2023 Global Scripture Access Study,* only around 10% of the world's 7,394 languages can access a complete Bible.[9] Artificial intelligence may conceivably be able to complete translations of the other 90% in our lifetimes—perhaps even in a generation.

Guideline 4: Embrace Positive Change

Since 2017, developers have explored using unsupervised machine learning to translate new languages. Matthew Hutson explains how it works:

> To start, each [method] constructs bilingual dictionaries without the aid of a human teacher telling them when their guesses are right. That's possible because languages have strong similarities in the way words cluster around one another. The words for table and chair, for example, are frequently used together in all languages. So if a computer maps out these co-occurrences like a giant road atlas with words for cities, the maps for different languages will resemble each other, just with different names. A computer can then figure out the best way to overlay one atlas on another. Voilà! You have a bilingual dictionary.[10]

Remember that this was almost seven years ago, a lifetime in the field of artificial intelligence. In 2023, a team of archaeologists and computer scientists made headlines after finding a way to use AI to translate 5,000-year-old Akkadian tablets.[11] It's still an early field, but it's developing at a rapid pace. Astonishing.

While this technology may significantly accelerate the translation process, there are still tricky hurdles ahead. Translation is a complicated process, and while AI *may* be able to handle a word-for-word translation, it could struggle with appropriately communicating the text's thought (or sense). In other words, AI may do well with formal equivalence but struggle with dynamic equivalence; the most popular/valuable Bible translations tend to strike a healthy balance between the two. But the technology is still young. The signs are promising.

2. AI for Multilingual Ministry

AI's language translation prowess will open doors that were previously bolted shut. At the time of writing, Meta's SeamlessM4T technology can understand audio or text in approximately 100 languages and use just one AI model to translate the input instantly into 36 different languages.[12] Google Pixel phones already have a "live translate" feature, and Samsung will reportedly be able to translate phone calls in real-time in 2024.[13] Products such as Rask can already translate audio from a video into a different language while maintaining the tone and timbre of the original voice.

Incredible.
What might this mean for churches?

There will undoubtedly be many opportunities for cross-cultural missions and greater support for first-generation immigrants with prohibitive language barriers. The current state of translational software recently afforded me the chance to converse with several Ukrainian immigrants who had only just arrived in Canada. Without these technological developments, such communication would've been impossible. It was incredible and, quite honestly, very moving. It's exciting to think about what advances in this field might bring, but this is only scratching the surface.

This technology will be especially transformative when combined with any form of extended reality (XR), particularly augmented reality (AR). The release of the Apple Vision Pro headset shows that "spatial computing" is viable, though its first iteration is perhaps too heavy and expensive to be widely adopted just yet. In time, such technology seems inevitable. Companies have been working hard on AR contact lenses,[14] but development costs have been prohibitive.[15] AI expert Kai-Fu Lee is optimistic, believing the technology will soon be affordable and widely adopted:

> Several start-ups are already working to develop XR contact lenses. Their prototypes show that displays and sensors can be embedded in contact lenses, making text and images visible. These contact lenses will still require external CPU for processing, which can be done on a mobile phone. By 2041, we anticipate the "invisibility" of contact lenses will truly cause the market to accept the product, and that challenges such as cost, privacy, and regulations will be overcome.[16]

Of course, AI isn't dependent on contact lenses to enter the AR space. XR devices like Mark Zuckerberg's Meta Quest 3 and the Apple Vision Pro show there are other avenues to the technology, but it's well within the realms of possibility that within a decade, humans could possess the technological capability for all believers to join together in worship, listening to a sermon in one language but seeing real-time subtitles on AR lenses. We're edging closer to the reality of experiencing multiple languages singing out in worship to the Lord together—one melody but many tongues. We're on the precipice of a moment in history where audio description and automated subtitles can improve accessibility to worship services for those with visual or hearing impairments.

Conversely, AR technology in glasses and contact lenses could be even more of a distractive force than smartphones, which is a concerning thought. However, we could find ourselves one step closer to that great future reality revealed to us in Revelation, where a great multitude "from every nation, from all tribes and peoples and languages" come before the throne together (Rev. 7:9). Of course, the technological capability to do something is not same as the financial viability to make it happen, but those days are drawing nearer.

3. AI for Administration

AI's ability to handle administrative tasks will be transformative for church management. It can free up valuable resources by automating routine tasks like scheduling volunteers, taking meeting minutes, managing finances, tracking attendance, and managing trends. AI can already code reasonably high-quality websites, edit (and indeed, create) photos, videos and audio, and provide the foundations for chatbots that help prospective visitors—who perhaps aren't ready to commit to meeting or messaging with someone—understand the church's vision and values. It could be, and in many cases already is being used to help with content creation and event advertisement.

Guideline 4: Embrace Positive Change

As we explored in the previous chapter, churches could spend fewer resources and considerably less time running the church and more on *being* the church. If the world is about to face the relational challenges we explored in Guideline 1, more shepherding and fewer logistical concerns would certainly be a good thing. The reality is that specific use cases of artificial intelligence in ministry administration are almost limitless and will perhaps have the most immediate impact on how Churches function.

The challenge with increasingly AI-driven administration is the lack of human connection in the organizational process. The church may be more efficient, but there could be fewer touchpoints for meaningful connection in the day-to-day activities and procedures inherent in administrative life.

4. AI for Outreach

There are equally varied ways in which artificial intelligence can assist churches in serving their cities. AI can help a church understand its context, demographics, and needs. As a result, they could potentially serve and evangelize their location more effectively.

A few months ago, our church hosted a winter clothing drive, meeting a specific felt need in our city, where temperatures can drop to around -40°C (which, if you're wondering, is the same in Fahrenheit). We received an enormous amount of clothing donations and had the opportunity to give stacks of jackets, hats, gloves, and scarves to those in need. This led to incredible opportunities to love our community and share the gospel. You might be surprised that ChatGPT played a big part in planning the event.

Let me share how this event materialized:

As a church, we knew God was leading us to help meet the needs of our community (Isa. 58:10; Matt. 25:35-40; Jam. 1:27), but we were struggling to find a way to do that. At a loss, I typed the following prompt into ChatGPT:

> We are a Christian church in Red Deer, Alberta. There are around 50 members in our church, and we meet in the downtown area. You will analyze the city's demographics and needs and devise a series of ways in which a church of our size and minimal resources may be able to meet those needs with an outreach event in the winter with one month's preparation.

The response was too large to copy word-for-word, but these sections were particularly intriguing:

> *Winter-specific needs:* Cold weather brings unique challenges, like the need for warm clothing, shelter for the homeless, and social isolation, especially among the elderly.
>
> *Event Ideas:* Warm Clothing Drive: Collect coats, gloves, hats, and scarves to distribute to those in need. Consider partnering with businesses for collection points.

This suggestion brought our "Wrap Up the City" event to life! Of course, ChatGPT didn't plan the whole event

Guideline 4: Embrace Positive Change

(although it did help with ideas for spreading the word). Nor did it put in hours upon hours of heartfelt prayer and hard work to make the event happen—that was thanks to our wonderful church community. However, ChatGPT helped identify a need particular to our city and season and helped to get the ball rolling in a valuable way.

In other contexts, AI could help optimize resource allocation (for example, in food banks), tailor sermon series to meet the location's needs, or provide invaluable help for ideation and administration. In terms of pure support for outreach, it could be hugely beneficial.

5. AI for Education

As we saw in the previous chapter, artificial intelligence could be both a blessing and a curse for education in general. But what about education in the Church? AI can cater to students' unique learning styles and paces through personalized algorithms, offering a customized educational experience. AI can also provide access to vast resources, facilitate interactive learning, and even assist in research and analysis in fields like textual criticism.

Kids may find their learning experience customized and gamified by AI in a way that is highly enjoyable and interactive, helping little ones to learn more about God while parents focus on helping their children to actually *know* him. On the other hand, as we've already seen, AI may render traditional education obsolete. It could radically lower financial barriers to entry for potential students, allowing anyone who senses a call to ministry to get the education they need at a manageable—perhaps even negligible—cost. Such changes could be significant in developing nations where the gospel is spreading like wildfire, but the financial resources for stellar training are not there. As we've already seen, Christian education may be able to give more focus to character development than intellectual preparation. This is no bad thing, given the number of controversies and fallen pastors in the last five to ten years.

6. AI in Worship

AI could significantly impact Sunday worship gatherings. The types of AR glasses and mixed reality headsets discussed above could mean that music teams see visual metronomes, lyrics, chords, and perhaps even sheet music right before their eyes, eliminating the need for music stands and charts. AI can already help with song selection and songwriting (though both require careful discernment and prayer) or help the worship leader find suitable passages to accompany a specific song.

The technological developments of the 2000s ushered in a renewed interest in backing tracks; you may not know this, but they are used by almost every well-known contemporary worship team today. At their best, this technology enabled smaller sung-worship teams to substitute the missing musicians for larger teams to add musical flourishes that weren't possible in most live circumstances.

Today, more and more companies are beginning to release AI music generators, and it's possibly only a matter of time before AI completely replaces backing tracks as we know them. Imagine a setting in the future where a worship leader can tell an AI engine what song they're playing and what key they're playing it in. This AI musician could provide an AI accompaniment in real-time, responding to dynamic and tempo fluctuations and perhaps even recognizing specific worship leaders' visual cues thanks to a combination of powerful image recognition capability and machine learning. It might even play multiple instruments at once!

Or picture an alternative scene: as a solo worship leader strums their guitar, they have a foot pedal with six options: acoustic guitar, bass, drums, electric guitar, keyboard, and "all in." While strumming, they can choose from any instrumental accompaniment they want, and—with a combination of pre-programmed and AI-driven technology—the worship leader could be supported by a full band while playing alone. Unlike the clunky, relatively inflexible versions of backing tracks available today, these AI instruments will be virtually indistinguishable from professional quality musicians.

This sort of technology could be profoundly helpful in the right setting and with the right approach. The question is whether AI can develop the creative abilities necessary to cope with such a task. The computational requirements of something like this are staggering but not insurmountable.

But there's more.

A world of possibilities could open regarding "visual worship experiences." Imagine reflecting on the empty tomb and seeing an AI-generated, immersive virtual experience so real it feels like you're right there. Or imagine the pastor being able to transport the congregation to the shores of the sea of Galilee as they reflect on the words of Jesus, or stand in the deserts of the wilderness, or amid the Areopagus gathering where Paul delivered his speech in Acts 17.

In a slightly nearer future, AI may allow for other technological developments such as dynamic, automated camera switching, AI-driven audio engineering, and presentation software that "hears" the songs as they are sung and changes the slides accordingly.

Yes, there would be less of a burden on volunteers. But of far more value is that more people who would have been volunteering in some capacity could concentrate on undistracted worship of God, welcoming newcomers, and cultivating relationships in the body of Christ.

How Can We Use These Opportunities for God's Glory?

Many people viewed technological breakthroughs with suspicion before they brought enormous benefits to the Church. In our quest to be technological semi-Luddites, it's important to recognize—with caution and discernment—the potential for AI to be a blessing to believers worldwide. From enhancing Bible translation to revolutionizing how we manage church operations and engage with our communities, AI presents once unimaginable opportunities, just as Guido D'Arezzo's musical notation system, the printing press, and the radio did in bygone eras.

There is a brave new world to explore—with cautious optimism—for the glory of God and the proclamation of the Good News of Jesus. Perhaps we'll be staggered by the kingdom fruit that grows out of these opportunities. But how do we distinguish between healthy opportunities and endeavors that could be detrimental to the body of Christ?

Reflection Questions for Guideline 4: Embrace Positive Technological Developments

1. What are some potential benefits of using AI in the church?

2. What are some possible pitfalls of using AI in the Church?

3. How can we use AI positively while ensuring it doesn't replace genuine human interaction?

4. How can we develop discernment both as individuals and as a church community to distinguish between beneficial and harmful applications of AI in the Church?

5. What are some potential applications of AI that directly contradict core biblical values and harm the body of Christ?

6. How can the church foster open and honest dialogue about the use of AI?

7. How might AI-powered tools be used to help with biblical training without becoming a distraction?

NOTES

[1] "Printing Press," *HISTORY*, last modified June 29, 2023, accessed August 16, 2023, https://www.history.com/topics/inventions/printing-press.

[2] Rudolf Hirsch, *Printing, Selling and Reading, 1450-1550* (Wiesbaden: Otto Harrassowitz, 1974), 1.

[3] Tom Wheeler, "With New Technology Challenges, Remember We've Been Here before," *Brookings*, last modified 2019, accessed December 7, 2023, https://www.brookings.edu/articles/with-new-technology-challenges-remember-weve-been-here-before/.

[4] John Foxe, "The Invention and Benefit of Printing (c. 1563)," in *The Acts and Monuments of John Foxe*, ed. Stephen Reed Cattley, vol. 3 (London: R. B. Seeley and W. Burnside, 1837), 718-22

[5] Mark Rogers, "Christian History: Broadcasting the Gospel," Christianity Today, last modified 2010, accessed December 7, 2023, https://www.christianitytoday.com/history/2010/march/broadcasting-gospel.html.

[6] Paul Matzko, "Meet the Pioneering Radio Preachers Who Revolutionized Religious Broadcasting," *ChristianityToday.Com*, last modified June 28, 2022, accessed December 7, 2023, https://www.christianitytoday.com/ct/2022/june-web-only/ministers-new-medium-fulton-sheen-walter-maier-radio.html.

[7] Ibid.

[8] "Some Pros and Cons: Shedding Light on Overhead Projection," *Reformed Worship*, last modified 1999, accessed December 7, 2023, https://www.reformedworship.org/article/march-1999/some-pros-and-cons-shedding-light-overhead-projection.

[9] "2023 Global Scripture Access," *Wycliffe Global Alliance*, 2023, accessed December 7, 2023, https://www.wycliffe.net/resources/statistics/.

¹⁰ Matthew Hutson, "Artificial Intelligence Goes Bilingual—without a Dictionary," last modified 2017, accessed July 26, 2023, https://www.science.org/content/article/artificial-intelligence-goes-bilingual-without-dictionary;

¹¹ Kevin Dickinson, "New AI Translates 5,000-Year-Old Cuneiform Tablets Instantly," *Big Think*, July 4, 2023, accessed December 8, 2023, https://bigthink.com/the-future/ai-translates-cuneiform/.

¹² Kristen Houser, "Meta's First-of-Its-Kind AI Can Translate between Any of 100 Languages," *Freethink*, August 31, 2023, accessed December 8, 2023, https://www.freethink.com/robots-ai/universal-translator.

¹³ Richard Lai, "Samsung Teases Its Own AI-Based Real-Time Phone Call Translation," *Engadget*, last modified November 9, 2023, accessed December 8, 2023, https://www.engadget.com/samsung-teases-its-own-ai-based-real-time-phone-call-translation-053818106.html.

¹⁴ Louis Rosenberg, "Huge Milestone as Human Subject Wears Augmented Reality Contact Lens for First Time," *Big Think*, July 6, 2022, accessed December 8, 2023, https://bigthink.com/the-future/augmented-reality-ar-milestone-wearable-contacts/.

¹⁵ Cromwell Schubarth, "Bay Area Startup Mojo Vision Puts Smart Contact Lenses on Hold, Cuts Staff by 75%," *Silicon Valley Business Journal*, last modified January 6, 2023, accessed December 8, 2023, https://www.bizjournals.com/sanjose/news/2023/01/06/saratoga-based-mojo-vision-cuts-staff-by-75.html.

¹⁶ Kai-Fu Lee and Chen Qiufan, *AI 2041* (New York: Currency, 2021), Kindle Loc. 3477 of 7291.

Guideline Five: Stay Informed in a Rapidly Changing Environment

Imagine artificial intelligence as a vast, unknowable ocean, incomprehensibly deep and distant, as capable of destroying life as cultivating it. At the Church and AI's intersection, you are Columbus, tasked with navigating, taming, exploring, and leading your people into uncharted territory. In the previous chapters, we've explored some of the necessary tools and resources to ready ourselves to set sail on this grand adventure. A plan is starting to form.

Your crew represents the importance of championing authentic, meaningful, and, most importantly, human relationships in a world more digitally connected but increasingly socially disconnected. Just as captains rely on loyal, well-coordinated, and tight-knit crews to navigate the seas, churches must prioritize relationships to manage the coming changes effectively.

Your ship is a symbol of the need to nurture resilient congregations. In the same way that a ship must be strong, hardy, and well-maintained to withstand the unpredictable seas, church leaders must prepare their congregations as best they can to weather the coming societal, cultural, and technological storms that loom on the horizon.

Your sails are a picture of the need for adaptable structures within the Church. Just as sails must stand firm in the face of powerful winds and waves, they must also be flexible to adjust course when necessary. Likewise, leaders would do well to cultivate within their congregations a semi-Luddite attitude towards technological changes: willing to stand firm against those destructive winds of change that imperil the Great Commission but simultaneously adaptable to the shifting sands and storms of this world.

Your tools reflect the need to embrace positive technological developments. Columbus embraced the most cutting-edge technology available to him in his day: tools like the magnetic compass and the astrolabe for celestial navigation. These technologies helped sailors to explore new territories with accuracy and precision. Similarly, when the Church embraces positive technological developments, leaders can discover new ways to venture into unexplored regions and effectively fulfill the Great Commission. In this chapter, we'll add another factor to this voyage.

Guideline 5: Stay Informed in a Rapidly Changing Environment

Let's continue our sea-faring analogy.

If you're a leader in your church community, consider yourself a captain. Your role is to observe the seas and skies constantly and use the most up-to-date nautical charts available to you to make good decisions for the sake of your crew (and your voyage). Just as a skilled mariner must understand and respond to the changing conditions of the sea, church leaders must stay informed about the changing world to guide their congregation wisely.

Staying informed about the developments in AI is a critical component of these seven guidelines. Depending on your personality type, it might feel too trivial or overwhelming to keep up with artificial intelligence's ever-changing and swirling seas. In the following pages, we'll seek to fight both extremes by asking two fundamental questions:

- Why should we stay informed about AI?
- How should we go about following this vast torrent of news?

Why Should We Stay Informed?

Perhaps a thousand different issues, topics, and pastoral concerns are floating around in your mind regarding the Church. Many of them require constant attention, possibly more than you can manage. Why should artificial intelligence be one of them?

The fact that you're reading this tells me that you have at least *some* interest in the subject. For the sake of your time, we won't cover all of the reasons to stay informed—those are topics worthy of another book, and there will likely be more by the time you're reading this—but below are some broad considerations. The following diagram will act as our **navigational chart**, starting with the smaller, more immediate reasons to stay informed and progressing to the larger, seemingly more distant ones.

Why Church Leaders should Stay Informed about AI

Guideline 5: Stay Informed in a Rapidly Changing Environment

Regarding AI, the Church must be proactive, not reactive.

Perhaps the most critical reason for the Church to stay informed in this rapidly changing world is to make *proactive* rather than *reactive* decisions in light of AI. As we'll see, artificial intelligence might be a Pandora's box that will be practically impossible to shut once opened. If church leaders can stay reasonably informed about the cultural, technological, societal, economic, existential, and ethical challenges looming on the horizon, they can adequately prepare to meet these changes head-on in a way that glorifies God and draws people to him.

The book of Proverbs celebrates the virtues of diligence and foresight, or, to put it another way, the need to be proactive rather than reactive. Consider the following examples:

Proverbs 6:6-8: "Go to the ant, you slacker! Observe its ways and become wise. Without leader, administrator, or ruler, it prepares its provisions in summer; it gathers its food during harvest."

Just as ants are self-motivated and proactive and prepare their provisions in periods of abundance, the church can be proactive in staying informed and preparing for the staggering changes that might be waiting for us in light of artificial intelligence.

Proverbs 21:5: "The plans of the diligent lead to profit as surely as haste leads to poverty."

A thoughtful, well-planned, and diligent approach to tasks and challenges is the path of wisdom. Similarly, by continually staying informed about the current state of AI, the Church can carefully plan its response and avoid reckless decisions. In so doing, leaders can proactively navigate the complexities of the technology in a way that honors the Lord.

Proverbs 22:3: "A sensible person sees danger and takes cover; the inexperienced keep going and are punished."

The author highlights the foresight of a sensible person who identifies and avoids danger. In the context of AI, the Church would similarly do well to be aware of the potential challenges and ethical dilemmas that AI might present and take proactive steps to mitigate risk. By engaging with AI early and keeping abreast of technological developments, the Church can offer well-reasoned, prepared responses that elevate God-honoring principles and biblical theology while advocating for an ethical, morally sound use of these technological advances. In doing so, believers can anticipate cultural shifts and minister effectively.

On the other hand, if the Church is *reactive* rather than proactive, its leaders may find they are continually scrambling to address the aftermath of technological developments, resulting in disconnects with the needs and realities of the community, especially younger, more technologically literate generations. A global Church disconnected from the needs of its community will inevitably lead to less fruit for the kingdom and perhaps further declines in church attendance.

Guideline 5: Stay Informed in a Rapidly Changing Environment

The Church must recognize and address societal issues.

Wise churches will pay close attention to the imminent cultural, economic, and technological changes that are taking place in our society. So far, this book has sought to convince you that increasingly advanced AI will utterly transform our culture and that this should be where the Church directs its primary focus regarding the issue. However, we can only respond to these changes when we *recognize* that they are even happening.

We've discussed how our digital presence is cannibalizing our physical and emotional ones and how, on its current trajectory, AI is set to make it worse. However, there are myriad other ways in which artificial intelligence could conceivably change our culture and societal norms. The last chapter showed how AI will likely transform education, although it's difficult to say whether it will be for better or for worse. As we have seen, AI-driven education can give us the kind of individual support we could have only dreamed of decades ago. But it might also be a distractive atomic bomb that disintegrates what little concentration a generation of digital natives were clinging to by their fingertips.

Furthermore, AI-based advances raise a vast gamut of ethical concerns that extend beyond relationships and education. For example, one significant area of contention making waves among news outlets involves copyright and intellectual property laws. As AI systems become more adept at generating creative content, what about ownership and attribution? Who owns the rights to work produced by an AI artist or music composed by an AI algorithm?

To what extent could either of these mediums even be considered art?

Beyond copyright, we must also contend with privacy protection, another critical issue in the coming years. With incomprehensible amounts of data collected and analyzed by AI systems, growing dissenting voices are raising legitimate concerns about how this information is used and safeguarded. However, the issues still go further, descending from unethical to outright illegal. Non-consensual deepfake pornography is on the rise, subjecting its victims to considerable trauma in the process; early 2024 saw a "first-of-its-kind AI heist," where a multinational company lost around $25 million to perpetrators utilizing deepfake technology.[1] Numerous stories are beginning to emerge of unethical operators attempting to scam people by cloning the voices of their loved ones using AI and misleading the victim into believing they have been taken hostage.

Note: If you haven't already, make sure that you and your loved ones share a "safe word" to ensure that it is really them that you are talking to.

AI is a black box filled with bias.

One of the major challenges with artificial intelligence in its present iteration is that it is practically impossible for humans to understand how it arrives at its conclusion. It's a problem commonly referred to as the "black box" issue. As users, we see the process's starting point and endpoint but not the innumerable decisions made to get there. These mechanisms vacuum up immense data, autonomously

Guideline 5: Stay Informed in a Rapidly Changing Environment

extracting patterns and principles without direct instruction or coding from humans. Neural networks might learn to recognize objects in pictures. In doing so, it trains *itself* to recognize distinctive criteria for, say, identifying a cat. The problem is that because of the black box problem, there is no way of knowing the precise characteristics of these criteria since they're concealed within the network's elaborate layers of neurons and nodes. For feline discovery processes, this isn't too concerning. But here's where the challenge lies:

- Imagine if an autonomous vehicle suddenly swerves and causes an accident. If we didn't understand the process that led to such an error, it would hinder improvements in safety protocols and erode public trust in autonomous technology.
- In a financial context, an AI-driven algorithm might start executing unfavorable trades based on misinterpreted market trends, leading to significant losses. Understanding the AI's decision-making process could be essential for mitigating such risks.
- In the healthcare sector, an AI diagnostic tool may incorrectly identify a patient's condition or recommend inappropriate—or dangerous—treatments, potentially jeopardizing patient safety and well-being. Understanding how the AI analyzes medical data and makes diagnostic or treatment suggestions is crucial for ensuring accurate healthcare delivery and minimizing the risk of medical errors at best and, at worst, death.
- An AI algorithm could inadvertently learn to associate sensational or fake news with higher engagement, leading to an increase in the spread of misinformation.

Therefore, AI systems could be responsible for nudging users toward the consumption of polarizing or factually incorrect content.

Ross Andersen highlights the problem in a fascinating article for the Atlantic:

> AI offers an illusion of cool exactitude, especially in comparison to error-prone, potentially unstable humans. But today's most advanced AIs are black boxes; we don't entirely understand how they work. In complex, high-stakes adversarial situations, AI's notions about what constitutes winning may be impenetrable, if not altogether alien. At the deepest, most important level, an AI may not understand what Ronald Reagan and Mikhail Gorbachev meant when they said, "A nuclear war cannot be won."[2]

While there is a burgeoning field dedicated to peeling back the layers of the AI black box and developing "explainable AI" (XAI), the complex nature of these decision processes means that it may be difficult to ever fully articulate the innumerable steps that lead to an AI's conclusion.

Another significant issue compounds all of this: bias in the machine's binary coding. It's unhealthy to anthropomorphize AI, but similarly risky to assume that AI is unquestionably objective in all its processes. Indeed, bias can manifest in multiple forms and at various stages of the process, thus potentially impeding a user's access to knowledge and

Guideline 5: Stay Informed in a Rapidly Changing Environment

meaningful interaction with the world. There are three primary sources from which bias can rear its head in artificial intelligence:

- **Training data:** An AI's decisions may exhibit bias when the dataset used to train a model is too narrowly focused. For example, if a medical diagnosis system trains on a particular demographic or geography, it might skew towards those conditions, even in patients from other demographics or locations where other factors could be at play.
- **Algorithms:** Bias in AI can also arise from the algorithm's design or the selection of specific variables and features within the model. For example, an AI-based credit assessment tool might overemphasize specific socioeconomic factors, such as postal codes or education levels. As a result, applicants could encounter biased outcomes where algorithms reject those from low-income backgrounds or lower levels of formal education who are otherwise perfectly trustworthy.
- **Humans:** AI systems can even reflect the biases of their human developers. The creators' conscious or subconscious prejudices and values can influence the AI system's programming and the choice of training data used. On the Lex Friedman Podcast in early 2023, Open AI CEO Sam Altman recognized this as an issue, discussing his concern about the bias of human feedback raters and the importance of avoiding "groupthink" bubbles that unduly influence the systems.[3] Fascinatingly, consumers on both sides of the political aisle have complained about oppositional bias

in LLMs such as ChatGPT and Google Gemini; in perhaps the most prominent case, the latter had to rescind its image generator after its CEO described the responses as "biased" and "completely unacceptable."[4]

As with the black box issue, serious efforts are underway to minimize bias, but eliminating it is exceedingly difficult—perhaps impossible. While AI boasts an impressive ability to gather information from innumerable sources, it can't entirely escape the challenges of bias for the above reasons. The result is that while AI can be beneficial, we must proceed with caution. "If," as John Lennox notes, "the ethical programmers are informed by relativistic or biased ethics, the same will be reflected in their products."[5] Users, beware.

Additionally, The Church must confront dangerous ideologies such as Transhumanism.

Transhumanism is an ideology that will undoubtedly warrant increasing discussion in the future. If the transhumanist movement continues towards its more extreme trajectories, the Church will be critical in leading people away from its more insidious objectives. As such, staying current with updates on these ideological visions is vital. Because of its uniquely challenging worldview, let's take a quick detour and explore the Transhumanist challenge; by doing so, we can better understand why staying informed of these changes is vital for us as the Church in the 21st Century.

Guideline 5: Stay Informed in a Rapidly Changing Environment

The False Gospel of Transhumanism

In many ways, artificial intelligence can be enormously positive for physical and mental health. AI should "enable researchers to unravel and master the vast complexities of human biology and thereby gradually banish disease."[6] The healthcare industry can cut costs, reduce errors with increasingly automated surgeries,[7] and perhaps even produce neural implant or human augmentation technologies "that will replace and improve [our] auditory perception, image processing, and memory."[8] While early iterations of this technology are almost universally positive, the transhumanists sit on the other, darker end of the extreme.

Fundamentally, transhumanists seek to use technology to improve human capability . . . but that's not all. Sachin Rawat's definition of the term is helpful, if a little troubling:

> Transhumanism is a philosophical movement that aims to free the human body and mind of their biological limitations, allowing humanity to transcend into a future unconstrained by death.[9]

As an idea, transhumanism isn't new. It's a concept heavily influenced by the Enlightenment belief that we can only achieve real progress through reason and science. Such an emphasis has, understandably, led to growing faith in the ability of technology to overcome the obstacles posed by the limitations of the human condition. The 20th Century also saw science fiction popularizing transhumanist thinking. As we've seen, Julian Huxley touched on the subject in

Brave New World, and it found an audience in *2001: A Space Odyssey* and even *Star Trek*. However, as we'll see, the transhumanist worldview has distant echoes of much older schools of thought.

But first, let's be clear here.

In many ways, aspects of this sort of thinking have been phenomenally positive for the human race. It's likely that you know someone who has had a hip or knee replacement (or two), cochlear implants to counteract hearing loss, or any number of technological enhancements to overcome the frustrations of our biological hindrances. Maybe you're even wearing glasses to read this book. The most extreme forms of transhumanist thinking simply push these ideas to their logical conclusions. In *God, Human, Animal,* Machine, Meghan O'Gieblyn notes, "We'll have similar neural-implant technologies that will replace and improve our auditory perception, image processing, and memory."[10]

So far, so good. It's difficult to argue with the possibility of improved memory; I'm sure my wife would be overjoyed if it meant I could find my wallet and keys more consistently. However, when we follow the thread to its furthest point, we face something more concerning. What O'Gieblyn writes next is startling:

> According to this thinking, consciousness can be transferred onto all sorts of different substrates: our new bodies might be supercomputers, robotic surrogates, or human clones. But the ultimate dream of

Guideline 5: Stay Informed in a Rapidly Changing Environment

mind-uploading is total physical transcendence—the mind as pure information, pure spirit. "We don't always need real bodies," Kurzweil writes in *The Age of Spiritual Machines*. He imagines that the posthuman subject could be entirely free and immaterial, able to enter and exit various virtual environments.[11]

If you're not concerned yet, keep reading. The next quote matters because, by some estimates, we might be there by the 2040s.[12] This is the heart of the transhumanist discussion:

> In his book *You Are Not A Gadget*, the computer scientist Jaron Lanier argues that just as the Christian belief in an immanent Rapture often conditions disciples to accept certain ongoing realities on earth—persuading them to tolerate wars, environmental destruction, and social inequality—so too has the promise of a coming Singularity served to justify a technological culture that privileges information over human beings. *"If you want to make the transition from the old religion, where you hope God will give you an afterlife,"* Lanier writes, *"to the new religion, where you hope to become immortal by getting uploaded into a computer, then you have to believe information is real and alive"* (Emphasis added).[13]

Wow.
You might need to read that again.
Slowly.

There is something profoundly troubling and inherently Gnostic about this perspective. Gnostics—an ancient group declared heretical to the Christian faith—sought to transcend the limitations of the material world through special knowledge.[14] In the same way, transhumanists seek to transcend the limitations of the human condition through special knowledge (and resultant technology). Both gnostics and transhumanists share the idea of "transcendence." Indeed, the ultimate goal is to move beyond the material altogether.

The similarities are startling, and ultimately, as prominent Church Fathers like Justin Martyr and Irenaeus noted in the first centuries after Christ's death, resurrection, and ascension, they are antithetical to the Christian faith. It's important to highlight that describing transhumanism as a genuine Gnostic heresy would be an overstatement. While there are echoes of the same reasoning, transhumanism is fundamentally secular.

However, there are still reasons for concern. Transhumanism is a false gospel. Here's why:

The true gospel of Jesus Christ teaches that we live in a fallen world damaged by the effects of sin and separate from a holy, loving God. (Gen. 3; Rom. 3:23). The just punishment for sin is death (Rom. 6:23). Jesus Christ, fully God and fully man, paid our debt on the cross and rose again, victorious over sin and death. Whoever trusts in Jesus can share that victory (1

Cor. 15:57), and are no longer bound by death. Instead, they will experience eternity in a restored relationship with the Lord God Almighty in heaven (John 3:16).

The counterfeit gospel of transhumanism tells us that we live in a fallen world where material realities are hindering us from experiencing life in all its fullness. One of these effects is death. We're told that artificial intelligence and the singularity will find a way for humans to live forever. Whoever believes in transhumanism and places their faith in a superintelligent, technologically produced knowledge will transcend the bounds of this broken world and experience eternity in an endless conscious existence.

There are similarities but some big problems. With transhumanism, humanity is trying to reach the heavens and make a name for themselves, dangerously excluding the omnipotent, incomprehensibly holy God of the Universe.

It's a 21st Century Tower of Babel.

As the Church, we *must* keep informed of developments regarding this expressly counterfeit gospel and prepare to engage with a world that may further lose interest in questioning the realities of life after death. From the perspective of an atheist, why should someone put their faith in Jesus for the *possibility* of eternal life when they could (in their minds) put their finances into a transhumanist organization and *guarantee* it?

From this vantage point, it is easy to see why people like American political scientist Francis Fukuyama describe transhumanism as one of the world's most dangerous ideas.[15] The body of Christ must stay informed, and shepherds must study these developments for the sake of their flock. We've already seen several challenging reasons why the Church must remain informed about AI. The final reason is perhaps the least likely but the most terrifying.

The Church must recognize and address the potential existential challenges of AI.

Earlier in this book, we saw the potential threats of artificial general intelligence (AGI) and heard the concerns of Stephen Hawking, Elon Musk, and even OpenAI's CEO, Sam Altman. After all, there's a reason that over 31,000 people signed an open letter recognizing AI's potential risks to society and humanity. We saw the risk of infrastructure profusion, where an AI might wreck the planet in pursuit of a singular goal, and the potential dangers of AI warfare. It certainly isn't beyond the realms of possibility that, in the quest to protect a nation, an AI system triggers nuclear war, with an opposing AI reacting in kind before a human even has time to blink. If such an event occurs, much of the Earth could be decimated before humanity realizes what's happening.

You might think, "Couldn't we just flick the power switch if AI goes haywire?" Or, "Why do AI experts feel that now is the time to sound the alarm?" The fundamental problem is that the world faces an arms race on two fronts:

- humans vs. humans, and
- humans vs. this hypothetical but eminently possible (and distantly looming) superintelligence.

Guideline 5: Stay Informed in a Rapidly Changing Environment

Calum Chace explains the challenges well in his book *Surviving AI*. Consider several poignant excerpts from his work:

> If there was a widespread conviction that superintelligence is a potential threat, could progress toward it be stopped? Could we impose "relinquishment" in time? Probably not, for three reasons.[16]
>
> ...First, it is not clear how to define "progress towards superintelligence", and therefore we don't know exactly what we should be stopping. If and when the first AGI appears, it may well be a coalition of systems which have each been developed separately by different research programmes.[17]
>
> ...Secondly, to be confident of making relinquishment work we would have to ban all research on any kind of AI immediately, not just programmes that are explicitly targeting AGI. That would be an extreme over-reaction.[18]
>
> ...The third reason why relinquishment is hard is the most telling. The incentive to develop better and better AI is just too strong. Fortunes are already being made because one organization has better AI than its competitors, and this will become ever more true as the standard of AI advances.[19]

Individuals, companies, and even nations may be left behind if they choose not to participate in artificial intelligence when others do, which is a worrisome prospect. Whether it's superintelligence, automated weaponry, economic advantages, totalitarian regimes, or any other potential issues, the biggest challenge is that it will take a united, concerted effort to reduce the risks. There have been *some* efforts to move in this direction, but certainly not enough for comfort. Thus, there are even more reasons why the collective body of Christ must stay vigilant in following the developments in AI. However, while existential crises are possible and worthy of attention, they are currently far from probable. In reality, Jesus will not return to a lifeless nuclear wasteland where humans have purged themselves from the landscape. Humanity *will not* be destroyed before God consummates his Master Plan, but that doesn't mean it's immune from irreparable damage. This sort of damage is clearly avoidable, but only if the Church takes these potential threats seriously and refuses to bury its head in the sand. We must stay informed in this fast-paced, ever-changing environment. But how can we do that?

How Can We Stay Informed?

The usage of the term "AI" reportedly quadrupled in 2023, resulting in its being named "Word of the Year" by dictionary publisher Collins.[20] Artificial intelligence is rapidly approaching ubiquity, making it increasingly difficult for anyone to keep pace with lightspeed changes. For this reason, before discussing the practical ways we can follow changes in the AI sphere, it's helpful to consider a healthy methodology

Guideline 5: Stay Informed in a Rapidly Changing Environment

for approaching the topic. Here are two suggestions:

1. Be informed about AI but not consumed by it.
2. Continually ask the question, "So what?"

Be informed about AI but not consumed by it.

So far, we've discussed why we should keep an eye on advances in artificial intelligence. Engaging with the general AI landscape is no bad thing, but it's important to maintain healthy boundaries and perspectives or risk becoming overwhelmed by the sheer torrent of data entering the news space daily. As we approach something resembling an "information apocalypse," where we are bombarded and overloaded with a range of legitimate, slightly questionable, and entirely fake news, we risk either becoming scared of the AI waters or drowning in them altogether.

Quite obviously, neither outcome is ideal. It's better to learn how to swim and humbly recognize our limitations while we do. Very few (if any) of us will sense the Lord's call to be experts in the intricacies of AI, and that's ok. However, it's wise to have enough understanding to gauge where the wind is blowing or—to continue with our water analogy—to understand how the tides are moving and currents are flowing.

Continually ask the question, "So what?"

With so much AI-related content in the news, it's easy to get lost in questions like, "How can AI automate my emails?" or the staple of Christian discussion, "Can/Should AI write my sermons?" Such questions aren't wrong; they're just the tip of the iceberg. Instead, consider asking, "So what?" Here are two examples:

Scenario 1 - Artificial intelligence can now accurately recreate your voice in multiple languages. **So what?**

- AI could take calls on your behalf, saving considerable time.
- This technology could open enormous opportunities for the gospel, as sermons and other content could be translated relatively effortlessly into myriad languages.
- However, the potential for fake news and disinformation may increase. In extreme scenarios, there is a heightened risk of scammers using the technology to pose as family members in fabricated hostage situations to extort money. Such a situation isn't scaremongering; it's happening even as you read this chapter.[21]

Scenario 2 - Artificial intelligence can now find your location in photos. **So what?**

- AI's ability to locate someone from a photo may be beneficial in emergencies, affording authorities an enhanced ability to find missing persons or quickly attend to accidents.
- It could also raise significant privacy concerns. Jay Stanley is a senior policy analyst at the American Civil Liberties Union; an article for NPR captures his concerns: Stanley worries that companies might soon

Guideline 5: Stay Informed in a Rapidly Changing Environment

use AI to track where you've traveled or that governments might check your photos to see if you've visited a country on a watchlist. Stalking and abuse are also obvious threats, he says.[22]

- On a cultural level, these concerns may lead to fewer natural photos and more with artificial backgrounds, exacerbating an already notable societal disconnect and, at worst, creating a digital world further removed from reality.
- There may also be implications for how organizations target markets with location-based advertising. Perhaps there's a future where you take a picture, AI recognizes your location, and immediately sends you an ad saying, "Hey! Are you hungry? There's a McDonald's a few blocks away. Click here for directions." If this is the case, the Church might consider utilizing this capability to advertise services but may find that doing so presents ethical challenges.

Of course, we could look at countless other scenarios. However, the point should be clear: by asking the "So What?" question, we can look beyond the surface level and explore the broader possibilities and challenges of a particular development in AI.

Practical steps for staying informed in an AI-driven world.

Here are some practical tips and resources for keeping up to date with developments in artificial intelligence:

- **Use curated resources.** Let someone else do the heavy lifting and give you a broad overview of what's happening in the field.

- **Engage in community discussions.** Because this field constantly evolves, consider holding semi-regular discussions in some format to explore the church's best response to ongoing developments. Such meetings could be inside or outside of your specific church context.

- **Use news apps to your advantage.** A reasonably basic but criminally underused feature of news apps is the ability to follow particular topics. For example, you might consider following "artificial intelligence" as a topic on your news app so you can wade through specific AI-related content on your phone or computer quickly and easily from various sources.

- **Set limits on your reading.** If you're anything like me, you might find yourself diving down a rabbit hole that's difficult to escape. The landscape of AI is changing on an almost daily basis. Set clear boundaries to avoid this.

- **Think critically.** AI is a booming field, meaning propaganda is rife. While asking the "so what?" question, also ask if there are any ulterior motives that might skew the news and proceed with caution.

For example, in late 2023, Nvidia CEO Jensen Huang boldly stated that computer scientists may attain

Guideline 5: Stay Informed in a Rapidly Changing Environment

artificial general intelligence (AGI) in the next five years. On the other hand, Yann LeCun, the chief AI scientist at Meta, is not convinced. Are these two differing but equal opinions, or is there more to the story? LeCun recently noted that "[If] you think AGI is in, the more GPUs you have to buy."[23] And who currently leads the way in supplying those GPUs? That's right: Nvidia, headed by Huang. Is this simply good salesmanship from the Nvidia CEO? Perhaps. It goes both ways: one might argue that LeCun is trying to appease shareholders himself. Whatever the reality of the situation, we must be careful with what we read.

Staying Informed in a Rapidly Changing Environment

There's much for us to process and plenty of reasons to see artificial intelligence as more than a fad. As we navigate ministry on the digital frontiers, we can best do so by understanding the landscape, constantly observing those tumultuous seas and cloudy skies, and making use of the best navigational charts we have available to us. In the next chapter, we'll see that all the information in the world is only as good as the wisdom accompanying it.

Reflection Questions for Guideline 5: Stay Informed in a Rapidly Changing Environment

1. How can we stay informed about artificial intelligence without becoming overwhelmed with the sheer volume of information?

2. What practical steps can individuals and churches take to stay informed about AI developments?

3. How can we discern between genuine AI developments and propaganda?

4. How might AI be problematic for churches regarding privacy, security, and human rights?

5. How should the Church engage with transhumanist thinking? How might you engage with the concept in your specific church context?

6. How should the church engage with some of the existential questions that arise regarding artificial intelligence?

7. How can we ensure that AI technologies are used responsibly and ethically within the church and broader community?

Guideline 5: Stay Informed in a Rapidly Changing Environment

NOTES

¹ Benj Edwards, "Deepfake Scammer Walks off with $25 Million in First-of-Its-Kind AI Heist," *Ars Technica*, last modified February 5, 2024, accessed February 14, 2024, https://arstechnica.com/information-technology/2024/02/deepfake-scammer-walks-off-with-25-million-in-first-of-its-kind-ai-heist/.

² Ross Andersen, "Never Give Artificial Intelligence the Nuclear Codes," *The Atlantic*, last modified May 2, 2023, accessed May 19, 2023, https://www.theatlantic.com/magazine/archive/2023/06/ai-warfare-nuclear-weapons-strike/673780/.

³ *Sam Altman: OpenAI CEO on GPT-4, ChatGPT, and the Future of AI | Lex Fridman Podcast #367*, 2023, accessed January 7, 2024 *Sam Altman: OpenAI CEO on GPT-4, ChatGPT, and the Future of AI | Lex Fridman Podcast #367*, 2023, accessed January 7, 2024, Sam Altman: OpenAI CEO on GPT-4, ChatGPT, and the Future of AI | Lex Fridman Podcast #367, 2023, accessed January 7, 2024, https://www.youtube.com/watch?v=L_Guz73e6fw

⁴ Dan Milmo and Alex Hern, "Google Chief Admits 'Biased' AI Tool's Photo Diversity Offended Users," *The Guardian*, February 28, 2024, sec. Technology, accessed March 16, 2024, https://www.theguardian.com/technology/2024/feb/28/google-chief-ai-tools-photo-diversity-offended-users.

⁵ Lennox, *2084: Artificial Intelligence and the Future of Humanity*, 149.

⁶ Kyle H. Sheetz, Jake Claflin, and Justin B. Dimick, "Trends in the Adoption of Robotic Surgery for Common Surgical Procedures," *JAMA Network Open* 3, no. 1 (January 10, 2020);

The study conducted by Sheetz et al. found that "the use of robotic surgery procedures increased from 1.8% to 15.1% from 2021 to 2018." It is reasonable to assume that this number is significantly larger today.

[7] O'Gieblyn, *God, Human, Animal, Machine*, Kindle loc. 771-773 of 3853.

[8] Rawat, "Transhumanism: Savior of Humanity or False Prophecy?," *Big Think*, July 27, 2022, accessed May 5, 2023, https://bigthink.com/the-future/transhumanism-savior-humanity-false-prophecy/.

[9] Ibid.

[10] Meghan O'Gieblyn, *God, Human, Animal, Machine* (New York, NY: Doubleday, 2021), Kindle Loc. 771-773 of 3853.

[11] Ibid.

[12] Kai-Fu Lee and Chen Qiufan, *AI 2041* (New York: Currency, 2021), Kindle Loc. 7198 of 7921.

[13] O'Gieblyn, *God, Human, Animal, Machine*, Kindle Loc. 1012 of 3853.

[14] Zachary G. Smith, "Gnosticism," ed. John D. Barry et al., *The Lexham Bible Dictionary* (Bellingham, WA: Lexham Press, 2016).

[15] Francis Fukuyama, "Transhumanism," *Foreign Policy* 144, no. Sep.-Oct., 2004 (2004): 42–43.

[16] Calum Chace, *Surviving AI*, Third Edition. (Three Cs, 2020), Kindle loc. 3311 of 4658.

[17] Ibid., Kindle loc. 3314 of 4658.

[18] Ibid., Kindle loc. 3322 of 4658.

[19] Ibid., Kindle loc. 3326 of 4658.

[20] Esther Addley, "'AI' Named Most Notable Word of 2023 by Collins Dictionary," *The Guardian*, November 1, 2023, sec. Technology, accessed December 17, 2023, https://www.theguardian.com/technology/2023/nov/01/ai-named-most-notable-word-of-2023-by-collins-dictionary.

[21] Justin Green, "Experts Warn of Rise in Scammers Using AI to Mimic Voices of Loved Ones in Distress," *ABC News*, last modified July 7, 2023, accessed December 19, 2023, https://abcnews.go.com/Technology/experts-warn-rise-scammers-ai-mimic-voices-loved/story?id=100769857.

[22] Geoff Brumfiel, "Artificial Intelligence Can Find Your Location in Photos, Worrying Privacy Experts," *NPR*, December 19, 2023, sec. Technology, accessed December 20, 2023, https://www.npr.org/2023/12/19/1219984002/artificial-intelligence-can-find-your-location-in-photos-worrying-privacy-expert.

[23] Jonathan Vanian, "Mark Zuckerberg Indicates Meta Is Spending Billions of Dollars on Nvidia AI Chips," *CNBC*, last modified January 18, 2024, accessed February 14, 2024, https://www.cnbc.com/2024/01/18/mark-zuckerberg-indicates-meta-is-spending-billions-on-nvidia-ai-chips.html.

Guideline Six: Be Proactive in Praying for God-Given Wisdom

Isaac Asimov once said, "The saddest aspect of life right now is that science gathers knowledge faster than society gathers wisdom."[1] Although it's been almost four decades since this statement was published, it's more pertinent than ever.

Knowledge is everywhere. Wisdom isn't.

What follows is an exploration of the strange, meandering road of knowledge and wisdom and its complicated relationship with artificial intelligence.

Guideline 6: Be proactive in praying for God-given wisdom.

In this chapter, we'll see how two ideas—relativism and subjectivism—have altered our relationship with truth. We'll explore how AI gives us greater access to information than ever, which is both an exciting and concerning reality. We'll address how combining AI issues and relativistic thinking presents believers with a serious wisdom problem that requires immediate attention. We'll look at what the Bible says about wisdom. Finally, we'll see why this means we must proactively pray for biblical wisdom in an increasingly AI-driven world.

How we respond to what follows might be one of the most important indicators of the Church's future health. Let's dive in.

Relativism, Subjectivism, and Our Relationship With Truth

Artificial intelligence hasn't developed in a vacuum. As we've seen, marked shifts in philosophical outlooks and sweeping technological changes have fundamentally shifted much of the cultural and socio-political landscape while AI was developing in the background. Two ideas we haven't paid much attention to—relativism and subjectivism—are essential in discussing the relationship between artificial intelligence, knowledge, and wisdom. It's helpful for us to consider two essential questions:

Guideline 6: Be Proactive in Praying for God-Given Wisdom

- What are relativism and subjectivism?
- How have these ideas risen to prominence?

Defining Terms

Relativism refers to the denial of objective or absolute standards, and it appears in several forms.[2] Proponents of *ethical* relativism believe that right and wrong aren't fixed, unchanging laws; instead, they are malleable and dependent on culture (cultural relativism) or personal preferences (moral subjectivism).[3] Few would dispute that someone's culture profoundly impacts how they live.

In this sense, we might broadly agree that there is *some* degree of cultural relativism in the world. The question is to what extent.

Although moral subjectivism is a subset of relativism, it's perhaps the most crucial definition in the context of this discussion. Moral subjectivism is an individual ethical relativism that "attempts to view what is normally thought to be objectively true or false as subjective."[4] In other words, according to moral subjectivists, what's true is open to interpretation based on personal experience and feelings.

This idea has far-reaching consequences. As Peter Kreeft writes (notably in opposition to this line of reasoning), ". . . only after the objective truth is denied are we 'free' to recreate new 'truths' in the image of our own desires."[5] When moral subjectivists reject objective truth, they inevitably seek to mold the world to their desires, irrespective of consequences.

Our contemporary culture is *steeped* in moral subjectivism. Perhaps you've noticed. But this is no new phenomenon. Socrates fought the relativism he saw in the sophists. With his student and protégé, Plato, the battle continued. He is said to have fought the views of Protagoras, a prominent sophist who believed that *man is the measure of all things*. In other words, individuals are the ultimate arbiters of truth in their world. For Plato, such a belief system couldn't stand. There had to be an eternal, objective Truth that transcends the world in which humans live.[6]

Notably, Plato's view has been the dominant perspective throughout the ages. In the 13th Century, the enormously influential Thomas Aquinas turned his attention to relativism, declaring that, as much as humans might try, one could never abolish the natural law from man's heart.[7] Importantly, this natural law wasn't a concept restricted to Western thought. C. S. Lewis was keenly aware of the *Tao*, a Chinese acknowledgment of a "reality beyond all predicates, the abyss that was before the Creator Himself... [a] doctrine of objective value, the belief that certain attitudes really are true, and others really false".[8] The *Tao* represents objective moral law rather than subjective values. Lewis uses the fascinating appendix of *The Abolition of Man* to illustrate the ubiquity of the *Tao* in cultures worldwide.

For a considerable time, minor factions questioned the objective nature of truth—though scholars argue that these factions perhaps weren't as dedicated to their cause as some would suggest. It wasn't until the work of Jeremy Bentham (1748-1832) and Georg Wilhelm Friedrich Hegel (1770-1830) that relativism began an ascent into the mainstream prominence it has found in the Western world today.[9] Nietzsche (1844-1900) followed these philosophers by questioning the view that there was an objective truth. Instead, he said, there are only *interpretations*.[10] It could well

Guideline 6: Be Proactive in Praying for God-Given Wisdom

be argued that Nietzsche espoused relativism in its purest possible form.

As someone who would have been keenly aware of the rise of relativism and witnessed the brutality of Nietzsche-inspired Nazism during the Second World War, C. S. Lewis viewed relativistic ideology with great concern. The horrors of war had scarred him, but he also saw that the effects of moral subjectivism spanned much further than war-mongering ideology. Lewis's *The Abolition of Man* arose in response to a book written by two schoolmasters (referred to as "Gaius" and "Titius") who were strong proponents of relativistic thinking. After reading their work, Lewis was distinctly unimpressed. As a keen student of history and a scholar who maintained a deep awareness of philosophers such as Bentham, Hegel, and Nietzsche, Lewis was well-positioned to refute Gaius and Titius' relativistic thinking. Perhaps unsurprisingly, Lewis approached the topic with a deftness and ability that few could match.

Though C. S. Lewis is best known for works like *The Chronicles of Narnia* and *Mere Christianity*, he actually dedicated much of his work to refuting the perils of relativism. In *The Poison of Subjectivism*, he summarizes the issue well:

> Until modern times no thinker of the first rank ever doubted that our judgments of value were rational judgments or that what they discovered was objective . . . The modern view is very different. It does not believe that value judgments are really judgments at all. They are sentiments, or complexes, or attitudes, produced in a

community by the pressure of its environments and its traditions, and differing from one community to another.[11]

Lewis could be writing for today's world. Indeed, those interested in delving deeper into Lewis's refutation of relativism might consider reading *The Poison of Subjectivism*, *The Abolition of Man*, *The Correspondance of C. S. Lewis and Don Giovanni Calabria*, *Bulverism*, *Mere Christianity* and *A Preface to Paradise Lost*. C. S. Lewis's writing is significant for contemporary readers who face the challenge of engaging with the subjectivism bombarding broad facets of everyday life.

Today, we find ourselves on the other side of an explosion in moral subjectivism and relativistic thinking; it's in everything from education to immigration policies, marriage laws, personal lifestyle choices, sexual proclivities, corporate marketing, faith issues, and critical race theory. If you've ever heard the phrase, "That's my truth," you're listening to a particularly egregious form of relativism in practice. It's a worldview that can be particularly damaging when combined with the growing individualism we saw in Guideline 1. In reality, the two ideologies are inextricably linked. Lewis shows the belief system to be logically incoherent at its very core—but that's a conversation for another day.

Now we've turned our attention to the 12,000 lb subjectivist elephant in the room, you might be wondering, "What does it have to do with AI?" We need to explore AI's complex relationship with information to answer that question well.

Guideline 6: Be Proactive in Praying for God-Given Wisdom

Artificial Intelligence and the Challenges of Information

As we've seen, the printing press fundamentally changed how people interacted with knowledge. The price of books plummeted, and as access drastically increased, information became more readily available than ever before. As recently as the early 1990s, libraries were the primary knowledge hubs of suburbia. With the early Internet, vast swaths of data entered the digital space. While rudimentary search engines existed, it wasn't until Google's algorithm-based system rose to prominence that humans gained greater access to the digital world. Google's endeavors were so successful that its *name* even became a verb! By the early 2000s, Google began incorporating machine learning into search with basic functions such as interpreting and correcting spelling mistakes. The tech giant then introduced Google Translate midway through the decade, further opening the door to the world's knowledge for everyone. Today, Google receives roughly 83 *billion* visits every month, making it one of the primary ways people access information.[12]

In the last few years, large language models (LLMs) have changed everything again. These LLMs can scour the Internet's information in seconds and synthesize it into a singular, (generally) coherent answer. Though still in its infancy, this breakthrough is astonishing. Experts in the field, such as Kai-Fu Lee, believe that in the next twenty years, LLMs like ChatGPT "will read every word ever written and watch every video ever produced and build its own model of the world. This all-knowing sequence transducer would contain all the accumulated knowledge of human history."[13]

In many ways, it's difficult not to be somewhat excited by the capabilities that allow humans to easily access unfathomably large streams of information. But that's been possible for a while. What makes AI so intriguing is its growing ability to give the perception of thinking and problem solving, an ability we're growing increasingly dependent on. We already rely on AI for online searches, grocery shopping, and deciding which show we should watch next on our favorite streaming service.[14] AI also helps coordinate our hospital systems, factory processes, and financial markets.[15] As artificial intelligence develops, it will become increasingly tempting for societies to consider AI the sole arbiter of knowledge, answers, and, dangerously, wisdom.

Church leaders aren't immune to this. LLMs can be incredibly helpful with, for example, certain facets of sermon preparation, administration, and pastoral care. However, while AI can be a useful support, it makes for a perilous crutch. At this point, our strive to be technological semi-Luddites comes to the fore once again. In some ways, these AI opportunities will be profoundly positive for our world. And yet, in others, this could be enormously problematic. Remember, AI is a black box filled with bias in the binary. Winston Churchill once commented, "We shape our buildings and afterwards they shape us." It's the same with technology. It'll undoubtedly be the same with artificial intelligence.[16] Perhaps we could refer to it as the "technological formativity of AI." As we shape AI, it'll shape us in return. It already has, whether or not we want to admit it. AI's personalization and recommendation systems, its distribution of information, its automated decision-making processes, and its various forms of bias that we saw in the

Guideline 6: Be Proactive in Praying for God-Given Wisdom

previous chapter are increasingly molding us. What do we do with all of this?

A Serious Wisdom Problem: More Knowledge, Less Truth

Fundamentally, we have entered a period where humanity has greater information but less objective truth than ever. As we depend more on AI for information, we find ourselves looking to systems with processes shrouded in enigma, inheriting bias from training data, algorithms, and developers, in a world where it's more difficult than ever to agree on what constitutes truth. Add that to everything we've discussed in the previous guidelines, and it's a potential recipe for catastrophic disaster. We're arriving at a juncture where knowledge is warped and skewed in myriad ways, making any question of pursuing wisdom exceptionally difficult.

From an evangelistic perspective, believers must point unbelieving friends and family toward logic, reason, and objective truth to lay a foundation for the Good News of Jesus. But that's a topic for another day. Before engaging with the world, we need to make sure we have a sound theology of biblical wisdom and pray God helps us stand on the objective truth of His Word in a subjectivist world.

So, what is *Biblical* wisdom?

Towards A Theology and Practice of Wisdom

On the silver screen, wisdom is almost always painted with the same broad strokes. Think of Yoda, Gandalf, Mister

Miyagi, Morpheus, Splinter, and Master Oogway, who regularly make internet "Top-Ten" lists as the wisest fictional characters ever written. These figures are remarkably similar: to varying degrees, they all bear the scars of age and are formidable warriors. They're disciplined, economical with their speech, and, in most cases, have an Asian influence. It's a revealing glimpse into the present-day secular view of wisdom. But are these the defining characteristics of the wise?

There are plenty of stereotypes about wisdom but few clear definitions. *Psychology Today* proposes that part of wisdom is "an optimism that life's problems can be solved" and that one can "experience a certain amount of calm in facing difficult decisions."[17] If this is the best definition that our psychologists can muster, clearly, there's a problem. What is *biblical wisdom*? Why should we pursue it? How do we get it? These are the sorts of questions we must wrestle with as believers if we want to engage with artificial intelligence well in the coming months and years. The following pages will propose that Biblical wisdom is a grace-given, awe-driven intimacy with God that results in Christlike character.

What is Biblical Wisdom?

Wisdom is more than *knowing* something, and it's certainly more than being able to fight with the age-defying prowess of Mister Myagi. Knowledge is the accumulation of facts, but wisdom is what you do with that knowledge. Brett McCracken explains it well in his book, *The Wisdom Pyramid*: "Wisdom is not merely knowing the right answers. It's about living rightly. It's about determining which right answer is best."[18] We have wisdom when we understand the challenges and complexities of life and possess insight to choose correct responses and behaviors in a given situation.

We might describe knowledge as a pantry full of ingredients. Wisdom isn't just knowing what's in the pantry; it's knowing which ingredients to use and how to combine them to cook something edible and nutritious. What makes biblical wisdom different if wisdom is the insight to use knowledge well? Paul explores this vital question in 1 Corinthians 1:20-25:

> Where is the one who is wise? Where is the teacher of the law? Where is the debater of this age? Hasn't God made the world's wisdom foolish? For since, in God's wisdom, the world did not know God through wisdom, God was pleased to save those who believe through the foolishness of what is preached. For the Jews ask for signs and the Greeks seek wisdom, but we preach Christ crucified, a stumbling block to the Jews and foolishness to the Gentiles. Yet to those who are called, both Jews and Greeks, Christ is the power of God and the wisdom of God, because God's foolishness is wiser than human wisdom, and God's weakness is stronger than human strength.

Paul is showing us there's a difference between *earthly* ideas of wisdom and *God's* idea of wisdom.[19] While some may consider God's wisdom little more than "foolishness," it's still infinitely more wise than any human wisdom, just as God's weakness surpasses any human strength. In other words, biblical wisdom is different from the world's wisdom.

But that's not all.

In 1 Corinthians 1:30, Paul tells believers, "It is from him that you are in Christ Jesus, who became wisdom from God for us—our righteousness." Jesus *became* wisdom for us. He's the very *personification* of wisdom. This incredible reality means that biblical wisdom is logically inseparable from Jesus and the life he led before Calvary. Whatever biblical wisdom is, it's certainly more than knowledge; it's different from the world's wisdom and inseparable from Jesus.

With these foundations in place, let's look to Proverbs, a book rich in insight and a critical guide for understanding biblical wisdom.

Proverbs 1:7: "The fear of the LORD is the beginning of knowledge; fools despise wisdom and discipline."

Proverbs 9:10: "The fear of the LORD is the beginning of wisdom, and the knowledge of the Holy One is understanding."

The phrase "fear of the LORD" refers to a sense of reverence and awe-struck wonder at who God is. Interestingly, such reverence toward God is the beginning of knowledge *and* wisdom, perhaps because we can grow in intellectual knowledge about God without necessarily *understanding* or knowing him personally. In other words, we can possess knowledge without wisdom, but we can't have wisdom without knowledge. Fools may know *about* God, but they can't put that knowledge into practice. But true wisdom and knowledge begin with a healthy fear of God's majesty. Ultimately, our perspective of God determines the direction of our life; the more we glimpse the enormity of the Lord God Almighty, the more difficult it becomes to do anything other than give all we have in worship to him. In *The Imitation of Christ*, Thomas à Kempis expresses this sentiment powerfully: "Vanity of vanities, all is vanity, save to love God, and Him only to serve. That is the highest wisdom, to cast the world behind us, and to reach forward to the heavenly kingdom."[20]

Biblical wisdom, therefore, is **awe-driven.**

When we're propelled by the sheer worship-inducing wonder of the Lord, the natural outcome is the pursuit of intimacy with Him (Psa. 63:1-3; Jer. 33:3; John 15:4-6; Jam. 4:8).

Biblical wisdom is an awe-driven ***intimacy with God.***

While a rightful fear of the LORD is a core component of biblical wisdom from which everything else grows, Proverbs still has plenty more to teach us on the subject:

Proverbs 14:6: "A wise person is cautious and turns from evil, but a fool is easily angered and is careless."
Proverbs 14:33: "Wisdom resides in the heart of the discerning; she is known even among fools."

As well as an appropriate perspective of God, biblical wisdom is cautious and discerning, turning away from evil.

Proverbs 11:2: "When pride comes, disgrace follows, but with humility comes wisdom."

Wisdom and humility are intricately connected. After all, if we strive to see the Ancient of Days in the fullness of his splendor, it will necessarily humble us!

Proverbs 12:15: "A fool's way is right in his own eyes, but whoever listens to counsel is wise."

Proverbs 13:1: "A wise son responds to his father's discipline, but a mocker doesn't listen to rebuke."

Biblical wisdom is knowing when to listen to the *right* people for appropriate counsel, discipline, and advice.

Do these characteristics remind you of anyone? Perhaps someone who turned from evil despite facing temptations in the desert? Perhaps someone who consistently showed patience and discernment? Perhaps someone who, being found in appearance as a man, humbled himself to death, even to the death of the cross? Someone who listened to the counsel of His Father, even though his perfection needed no discipline? When we pursue the sort of biblical wisdom outlined in the Proverbs and elsewhere in the Scriptures, the inevitable outcome is that we will become more like Jesus in our attitudes and actions. Biblical wisdom is an awe-driven intimacy with God that *results in Christlike character.*

Why Should We Pursue Biblical Wisdom?

If biblical wisdom is an awe-driven intimacy with God that results in Christlike character, the motivation for pursuing it seems reasonably self-explanatory: because we want to become more like Jesus. But if you're not entirely convinced yet, what else does the Bible teach us about the importance of pursuing biblical wisdom?

Proverbs 1:33: "But whoever listens to me will live securely and be free from the fear of danger."

Biblical wisdom aids us as we strive to live in this broken world. It leaves us secure in the knowledge that the Lord is with us, and our security is eternally found in Him alone, whatever the storms of this life bring. Biblical wisdom brings with it immense confidence.

Proverbs 3:13-18: "Happy is a man who finds wisdom and understanding, for she is more profitable than silver, and her revenue is better than gold. She is more precious than jewels; nothing you desire can equal her. Long life is in her right hand; in her left, riches and honor. Her ways are pleasant, and all her paths, peaceful. She is a tree of life to those who embrace her, and those who hold on to her are happy."

Biblical wisdom is worth far more than gold. It's far more valuable than anything that we could possibly desire in this world because it brings long life, riches, honor, happiness, and peace. These are principles, not promises, contrary to the anti-biblical teachings of the prosperity gospel.

For example, we know that, as a general rule, we'll become increasingly wealthy if we handle our finances well. However, unforeseen circumstances sometimes cause financial difficulties irrespective of our prudence (for example, a medical emergency, a house fire, or the effects of war). Similarly, if we live wisely toward others, we'll experience fewer arguments, confrontations, and stress. Yet many of us still deal with challenging relationships regularly.

When we recognize that the Proverbs are principles rather than promises, we can pursue biblical wisdom because it builds our confidence to persevere and increases our chances of finding riches, honor, happiness, and peace. But there's still more:

Proverbs 15:7: "The lips of the wise spread knowledge, but the heart of fools is not upright."

When we pursue biblical wisdom, our words will spread the sort of knowledge that can lead others to wisdom. It's the overflow of an upright heart close to God.

Proverbs 28:26: "The one who trusts in himself is a fool, but the one who walks in wisdom will be safe."

Those pursuing biblical wisdom find safety in knowing they are not dependent on their knowledge or strength. Instead, quite the opposite is true: to walk in wisdom is to trust the Lord above all else.

Proverbs 3:5-8: "Trust in the LORD with all your heart, and do not rely on your own understanding; in all your ways know him, and he will make your paths straight. Don't be wise in your own eyes; fear the LORD and turn away from evil. This will be healing for your body and strengthening for your bones."

A clear picture is emerging.

There is enormous value to pursuing biblical wisdom because when we find it, we find security and confidence in the Lord God Almighty, irrespective of what the world throws at us. Generally speaking, we'll find the sort of happiness and fulfillment that Jesus describes in his Sermon on the Mount. We become spreaders of knowledge and truth that can draw others to wisdom and arrive at a place where we can trust in God's power, understanding, and provision, knowing that he is walking with us every step of the way.

How Do We Grow in Wisdom?

It's all well and good to understand what biblical wisdom is and why we should pursue it. However, our next question must be practical: how do we attain it? Here's what the Lord shows us in his Word:

Proverbs 2:6: "For the LORD gives wisdom; from his mouth come knowledge and understanding."

Wisdom *comes from God*. Because biblical wisdom fundamentally differs from earthly wisdom, it makes perfect sense that it's God-given.

Proverbs 13:20: "The one who walks with the wise will become wise, but a companion of fools will suffer harm."

Although wisdom comes from God, we'll also grow in it when we spend time with wise people because, as Paul reminds us, "bad company corrupts good morals" (1 Cor. 15:33).

Proverbs 11:2: "When arrogance comes, disgrace follows, but with humility comes wisdom."

This statement is worth repeating: When we possess an awe-driven intimacy with God, it will *necessarily* humble us as we realize how much we pale compared to the God of all Creation. We are humbled as we comprehend the extent to which we are sinners in need of our loving God's forgiveness and how, in our strength, we're doing little more than fumbling around in the dark.

Wisdom comes from God as the result of a rightful awe and reverence towards Him. It comes to those who proactively seek it, walk closely with others who can help point them to it, and live with a humble recognition of their need for more of it.

But there is one final piece to the puzzle of biblical wisdom:

Biblical wisdom is a ***grace-given***, awe-driven intimacy with God that results in Christlike character.

Guideline 6: Be Proactive in Praying for God-Given Wisdom

It's impossible to find true biblical wisdom on our own. However, by God's grace, we live in light of the life of Jesus, fully man and fully God, filled with heavenly wisdom (Matt. 15:54). After a sinless, wisdom-filled life, he humbly gave himself over to death on a cross, rose again on the third day and ascended to be at the right hand of the Father. In doing so, he won the ultimate victory, conquered sin and death, and obliterated the great divide between Creator and creation. He was the atoning sacrifice for our sins, meaning whoever believes in and turns to Him shall not perish but have eternal life.

This is the gospel.

And the beauty of this good news is that we can find true biblical wisdom only through the grace-given gift of Jesus. In our strength, it would perpetually allude us.

A Call to Proactive Prayer for God-given Wisdom

In light of everything we've discussed, it's now time to return to the topic of artificial intelligence.

As believers, we venture into the digital frontiers at a time when our world has more knowledge than ever before but is less interested in objective truth than perhaps at any other time in history. We shape our technology, and in return, it shapes us. AI is no different. We're Frankensteins, creative scientists who have engineered something we don't fully understand. If we're not plagued by the technological formativity of the monster we've created, we soon will be.

While we load the machine with increasingly relativistic datasets and the inherent bias of its developers, it seems inevitable that it will soon turn the tables on us. We're at risk of being crushed under the weight of information overload. We're at risk of being led astray by the systems' mostly subtle—and sometimes not so subtle—bias. We risk blissful ignorance in the process as AI operates within its opaque and enigmatic black box.

We live in a world with lots of knowledge but not much truth; we're standing on the precipice of a wisdom crisis. For this reason, believers must proactively pray that God will equip us with the wisdom we so desperately need to fill the void. Biblical wisdom is a grace-given, awe-driven intimacy with God that results in Christlike character.

When we pursue God-given wisdom, we'll find objective truth in a worryingly subjective world. We can build our house on the rock and weather the incoming storms, however tumultuous. We can cut through the noise and proclaim the way of hope even when the calls to dangerous living seem loudest. We can look to God over and above the distractions and help others to do the same. We can implement AI into the life of the Church as a tool and not a crutch.

And this is good news for a changing world.

Reflection Questions for Guideline 6: Proactively Pray for God-Given Wisdom

1. How do you see the relationship between knowledge and wisdom today, particularly in light of AI?

2. How has/will AI change our relationship with information? What are the implications of using AI as a primary source of knowledge?

3. Reflect on the statement, "We shape our technology, and in return, it shapes us." How have you observed technology influencing human behavior?

4. Reflect on the phrase, "Biblical wisdom is a grace-given, awe-driven intimacy with God that results in Christlike character."

5. What is the Church's role in promoting wisdom and discernment in a world inundated with information?

6. What are some potential strategies for equipping believers to critically evaluate information and discern truth in an era of digital misinformation?

7. Reflect on AI as a "tool and not a crutch" for the Church. How can we maintain healthy relationships with technology while prioritizing spiritual growth and discernment?

NOTES

[1] Isaac Asimov, *Book of Science and Nature Quotations*, ed. Isaac Asimov and Jason A. Schulman (New York, NY: Weidenfeld & Nicolson, 1988), 280.

[2] Stephen C. Evans, "Relativism," in *Pocket Dictionary of Apologetics & Philosophy of Religion* (Downers Grove: Inter-Varsity Press, 2002), 101.

[3] Scott B. Rae, *Moral Choices: An Introduction to Ethics*, Third Edit. (Grand Rapids, MI: Zondervan, 2009), Kindle Loc. 276.

[4] Stephen C. Evans, "Subjectivism," in *Pocket Dictionary of Apologetics & Philosophy of Religion* (Downer's Grove, IL: Inter-Varsity Press, 2002), 111.

[5] Peter Kreeft, *C. S. Lewis for the Third Millenium: Six Essays on the Abolition of Man* (San Francisco, CA: Ignatius Press, 1994), 79.

[6] Plato, "Theaetus," 170a-171c.

[7] Thomas Aquinas, *Summa Theologica*, 2.94.6.

[8] C S Lewis, "The Abolition of Man," in *The Complete C. S. Lewis* (Toronto: McClelland & Stewart, 2014), Kindle Loc. 10994.

[9] "The Sophists," *Stanford Encyclopedia of Philosophy*, last modified September 30, 2011, accessed June 25, 2022, https://plato.stanford.edu/entries/sophists/.

According to the Stanford Encyclopedia of Philosophy, Protagoras is the only sophist to whom ancient sources ascribe relativistic views, and even in his case, the evidence is supposedly ambiguous.

[10] Louis Markos, *From Plato to Christ: How Platonic Thought Shaped the Christian Faith* (Downer's Grove, IL: IVP Academic, 2021), 272.

[11] C S Lewis, "The Poison of Subjectivism," in *Christian Reflections*, ed. Walter Hooper (Grand Rapids, MI: William B. Eerdmans Publishing Company, 1967), 90.

[12] "Google.Com Traffic Analytics, Ranking Stats & Tech Stack," *Similarweb*, accessed January 6, 2024, https://www.similarweb.com/website/google.com/.

[13] Kai-Fu Lee and Chen Qiufan, *AI 2041* (New York: Currency, 2021), Kindle loc. 2085 of 7291.

[14] Calum Chace, *Surviving AI*, Third Edition. (Three Cs, 2020), Kindle loc. 597 of 4658.

[15] Ibid., Kindle loc. 593-618 of 4658.

[16] John Frederick and Eric Lewellen, eds., *The HTML of Cruciform Love: Towards a Theology of the Internet* (Eugene, OR: Pickwick Publications, 2019).

The general theme of these collected essays was helpful in highlighting the fact that we shape technology, but in turn, it shapes us.

[17] "Wisdom," *Psychology Today*, accessed April 19, 2023, https://www.psychologytoday.com/us/basics/wisdom.

[18] Brett McCracken, *The Wisdom Pyramid* (Wheaton, IL.: Crossway, 2021), 66.

[19] Bruce B Barton et al., *Life Application New Testament Commentary* (Wheaton, Ill.: Tyndale House Publishers, 2001), 654.

[20] Thomas a Kempis, *The Imitation of Christ*, trans. William Benham, 1886.

Guideline Seven: Keep an Undistracted Focus on the Church's Mission

In September 1966, televisions in homes all over the USA rang out with the trills of a bassoon, followed by the staccato hits punctuating one of cinema's most immediately recognizable themes. A lit fuse burns across the center of the screen before the words "Mission: Impossible" announce a new spy show's dramatic arrival. Over six decades, what began as an unknown pilot has firmly established itself as an iconic brand, spanning multiple seasons on TV and almost thirty years of Tom Cruise-helmed movies. I've always loved one line in particular: "Your mission, should you choose to accept it..." Incidentally, the original line was "Should you *decide* to accept it," but the idea is still the same. It's a fascinating line because, as far as I'm aware, no one has ever refused to accept a mission! It's a detail that makes me wonder if there was a particularly short episode on the cutting room floor where Briggs or Hunt said, "Actually, I'll sit this one out. Come back when you've something less, well, impossible."

As the Church, our mission is different. In our strength, it's impossible. With God, mission success isn't just possible; it's *inevitable*. What's more, Jesus didn't leave believers with any doubt as to whether there was an opt-in for the mission.

There wasn't.
　There isn't.
　　It's a command.
　　　An imperative.

"Your mission, believer, whether or not you accept it. . ."

On the precipice of profound cultural shifts, it's easy for Christians to lose focus on the Church's mission. Possible existential realities of a world steeped in AI may dominate your thoughts. Or perhaps you feel disheartened by the rapidly changing landscape of our time and the crumbling of comfortable societal norms; after all, we live in a post-Christian culture, and that's still a tough pill for some to swallow. Or maybe you're reading this book with unbridled optimism, filled with excitement at the possible opportunities presented by AI, and desperate to capitalize on the nascent potential of this technology.

Let's be clear: both sentiments have a place, so long as they don't cause us to lose focus on the call of God on our lives.

Our seventh and final guideline for the body of Christ in

Guideline 7: Keep an Undistracted Focus on the Church's Mission

an AI-driven world is perhaps one of the most important: to keep an undistracted focus on the mission of the Church. This guideline is critical for a healthy journey into a future shaped by artificial intelligence. But what is the mission of the Church? In fact, what is the Church?

What is the Church?

At its most basic, we might say that the Church is the gathering of believers united under the leadership and authority of Jesus Christ, who is its head (Eph. 5:22-25; Col. 1:18). Gathering is of vital importance; the word "church" is translated from the Greek word *ekklēsia*, which literally means "assembly."[1] However, a mere assembly of like-minded people does not make the Church distinct. In *The Church: The Gospel Made Visible*, Mark Dever highlights the importance of the *ekklēsia* and what it means for believers:

> The church should be regarded as important to Christians because of its importance to Christ. Christ founded the church (Matt 16:18), purchased it with his blood (Acts 20:28), and intimately identifies himself with it (Acts 9:4). The church is the body of Christ (1 Cor 12:12, 27; Eph 1:22-23; 4:12; 5:20-30; Col 1:18, 24; 3:15), the dwelling place of his Spirit (1 Cor 3:16-17; Eph 2:18,22; 4:4), and the chief instrument for glorifying God in the world (Ezek 36:22-38; Eph 3:10). Finally, the church is God's instrument for bringing both the gospel to

the nations and a great host of redeemed humanity to himself (Luke 24:36-38; Rev 5:9).[2]

Clearly, the Church plays a vital role in the plans and purposes of the Lord. But the Bible is also rich in metaphors describing its nature; to focus on just one (i.e., the body of Christ) misses something of the Church's multifaceted nature. It's also described as Christ's bride (Eph. 5:25-27; 2 Cor. 11:2; Rev. 19:7-9; 21:1-2), highlighting Jesus's profound love for the Church and its call to purity and holiness. The Church is a summation of the gathered branches of Jesus, the true vine (John 15:1-5). It's the collected members of God's household, built on a foundation where Christ is the cornerstone (Eph. 2:19-20). While most Christians are confident that Jesus is the *reason* for gathering, we can sometimes forget just *how* central he is to the Church. Jesus is the founder, the head, the husband, the vine, the cornerstone, and the redeemer of the *ekklēsia*, which is also his body. While it's crucial to recognize the importance of *gathering*, it's also essential to acknowledge Christ's centrality in all facets of the church's expression.

The Church is visible and invisible, local and universal. Robert Letham describes the visible (or local) church as "the church here in this world, as an organism and an institution," whereas the invisible (or universal) church "consists of the entire company of the elect in all ages (Rev. 7:4-17).[3] It's invisible in the sense that it consists "not only of believers alive now but also of those who have died, those yet to profess faith, and those yet to be born."[4]

Guideline 7: Keep an Undistracted Focus on the Church's Mission

Whether we're discussing the visible or the invisible Church, its mission remains the same. But what is it?

What is the Mission of the Church?

Unlike the "Impossible Mission Force," genuine followers of Jesus don't have the opportunity to accept or reject the Church's mission. As such, it helps to know *what* that mission is. It's not as simple as we might first think; theologians throughout the ages have differed on the scope and focus of the Church's mission for generations. This chapter won't provide an exhaustive theological treatise on the subject but rather will give a broad overview informing us as we navigate the world of AI. It's also important to recognize from the start that as the body of Christ today, we can sometimes conflate the holistic mission of the Church with *missions* and *missionaries*. Missions—the specific initiatives or endeavors to spread the gospel or provide humanitarian support, often in cross-cultural contexts—are vital. But they are one part of the Church's overarching mission, not the whole.

If we are to understand the Church's mission, it's perhaps most helpful to start broadly and grow increasingly specific. In their excellent book, *What is the Mission of the Church* (which understandably offers a much more in-depth look at the subject), Kevin DeYoung and Greg Gilbert provide the following definition:

> The mission of the church is to go into the world and make disciples by declaring the gospel of Jesus Christ in the power of the Spirit and gathering these disciples into

churches, that they might worship the Lord and obey his commands now and in eternity to the glory of God the Father.[5]

It's a comprehensive statement and one of the best definitions of the Church's mission that I could find. However, for reasons that will become apparent, I propose the following (slightly more succinct) change:

> The Church is comprised of gathered believers called to fulfill Jesus' Great Commission, in the Spirit's power, to bring about the glorious worship of God the Father.

Although this statement contains only twenty-seven words—exactly half the length of DeYoung and Gilbert's statement—there is still a lot to unpack. Let's explore each of the component parts of this mission statement, starting at the end:

". . . and bring about the glorious worship of God the Father."

Worship is the ultimate calling of the human race. Almost 500 years ago, the Westminster Shorter Catechism correctly stated, "Man's chief end is to glorify God and enjoy him forever." Indeed, in *Desiring God*, John Piper famously pressed the case for what he calls "Christian Hedonism," arguing that "The chief end of man is to glorify God *by* enjoying him forever" (emphasis added).[6] In a later work, *Let*

Guideline 7: Keep an Undistracted Focus on the Church's Mission

the Nations Be Glad!, he reflects on the purpose of the church: "All of creation, all of redemption, all of history is designed by God to display God. That is the ultimate goal of the church."[7]

Piper's focus on worship is well-founded in Scripture. 1 Corinthians 10:31 commands believers to do everything for the glory of God. Ephesians 3:21 declares, "to him be glory in the church and in Christ Jesus to all generations, forever and ever. Amen." God—the one who is able to do above and beyond all that we ask or think according to the power that works in us—is to receive worship-fueled glory from the body of Christ. When asked what was the greatest command in the law, Jesus replied, "Love the Lord your God with all your heart, with all your soul, and with all your mind" (Matt. 22:37). In Revelation 7:11-12, the angels, elders, and four living creatures fall facedown before God, proclaiming:

> Amen! Blessing and glory and wisdom
> and thanksgiving and honor
> and power and strength
> be to our God forever and ever. Amen.

If that's the response of those at the Great Tribulation, we can reasonably infer that the Lord is worthy of a similar response from those he calls his children and coheirs with Christ today (Rom. 8:16-17).

Our role as the Church is to bring about the glorious worship of God the Father in as great a measure as possible. Our objective is to make much of the Lord, striving to bring him glory in whatever we do. Worship is a necessary response to a rightful view of God. A personal, corporate, and evangelistic component exists to accomplish this purpose. We give the Lord our worship individually by living sacrificially in view of his mercy (Rom. 12:1); we worship the Lord as a gathered body of Christ by meeting together as the *ekklēsia;* and we endeavor to fulfill the Great Commission with the express purpose of drawing more people toward giving the Lord the glory and honor that he rightfully deserves.

Let's explore that last point in more detail:

". . . to fulfill Jesus' Great Commission. . ."

If bringing glory, praise, and honor to the Lord is our primary objective, the Great Commission (Matt. 28:18-20) is not far behind and a crucial part of our expression of worship to the Lord:

> Jesus came near and said to them, "All authority has been given to me in heaven and on earth. Go, therefore, and make disciples of all nations, baptizing them in the name of the Father and of the Son and of the Holy Spirit, teaching them to observe everything I have commanded you. And remember, I am with you always, to the end of the age."

Jesus immediately reminds believers of his centrality to the Church's mission; after all, he is the one with *all* authority. In light of Jesus' divine prominence, our call is to go and make disciples until such a time that *all nations* become filled with them. Some churches inadvertently interpret making disciples as making converts, which can sometimes give rise to a focus

Guideline 7: Keep an Undistracted Focus on the Church's Mission

on seeker-sensitive gatherings. Evangelism is vital to making disciples, but it's just one part of the process. Discipleship begins the moment a person has committed to follow Christ. D. A. Carson describes disciples as "those who hear, understand, and obey Jesus' teaching."[8] Discipleship is more than simply believing in Jesus. It's the process of being nurtured and led by the Holy Spirit and other believers to grow spiritually and work out our faith daily. The ultimate purpose of making disciples is to help believers gain a rightful perspective of God in light of the gospel and cultivate a desire to delight themselves in glorifying the Lord in all they do. Baptism, explicitly mentioned in the Great Commission, is an essential step on this journey. It's an outward expression of the heart change that has taken place within.

The next section of the Great Commission is all too often overlooked in our contemporary age, much to the detriment of the Church: "... teaching them to observe everything I have commanded you." The Church's primary purpose is indeed to glorify him, as we have seen. It's also true that a crucial but secondary purpose is to make disciples of all nations, baptizing them in the name of the Father and of the Son and of the Holy Spirit. However, we must not forget the imperative to teach disciples to observe all Christ commanded us in the process. Jesus taught us that if we love him, we'll keep his commands (John 14:15)—but what are they? Consider the following:

- We've already seen the first half of the greatest command. The second half calls believers to "love your neighbor as yourself" (Matt. 22:39).
- We're called to serve the poor and the needy (Matt. 25:35-40; Luke 4:16-19; 14:12-14).

- We're called to pursue peace, justice, and compassion (Matt. 5:9; Luke 10:25-37; Luke 11:42).
- We're called to forgive others (Matt. 6:12, 14; 18:21-35).
- We're called to live with humility (Matt. 18:4).
- We're called to live with faith (Matt. 17:20; John 3:16-17).
- We're called to pray (John 14:13-14).

This brief list shows us that the Great Commission is *even more* than a call to make and baptize disciples in all nations. Indeed, we could extend this idea further by recognizing that since Jesus is fully God, every page of Scripture constitutes his Word and, by extension, his commands. When we live in line with biblical values and pursue righteousness for the sake of our great God, we're already working towards observing everything that Jesus has commanded us. The next part of this proposed mission statement builds on this important truth:

" . . . in the Spirit's power . . ."

We must recognize that keeping the imperatives laid out for us through Jesus' teaching and in the rest of the Scriptures in our own strength is impossible. We're simply too riddled with sin and marked human limitations in wisdom, understanding, strength, and resources. As we've already seen, God's wisdom differs from human wisdom. Similarly, while we can sow and water faith seeds for the sake of the gospel, it's only God who brings the growth (1 Cor. 3:6-7). Were we to go it alone, we'd join the spiritual equivalent of that Impossible Mission Force. The fuse would be lit, and the bassoon would start trilling, but we wouldn't get far. The mission would, quite literally, be impossible.

Thankfully, Jesus called us to pursue the Great Commission in the power of the Holy Spirit (Acts 1:8). Since Pentecost, the Holy Spirit has filled believers, dwelling in us (Acts 2:1-4; 1 Cor. 3:16) and guiding us into all truth (John 16:13). The gospel is proclaimed in power and in the Holy Spirit (1 Thess. 1:5), and believers can effectively engage in the great mission of God with the Spirit's fruit (Gal. 5:22-23) and gifts (1 Cor. 12:4-11; Rom. 12:6-8; Eph. 4:11-12) to help fulfill their divinely-inspired objective. Put simply, while the mission is great, the Spirit who empowers us is greater. In his strength, the mission is eminently possible. The Church is comprised of gathered believers called to fulfill Jesus' Great Commission, in the Spirit's power, and bring about the glorious worship of God the Father.

The Specific Call of the Church

We have defined the broad, overarching mission of the body of Christ, which is important. But it's also helpful to mention specific objectives that are key to fulfilling that mission. We've alluded to some already, and while they are subservient to the overarching goal, they are nevertheless important:

We're Called to Preach the Word and Administer the Sacraments.

The 16th century gave rise to the Protestant Reformation, which began a renewed focus on the Church's mission.

Article XII of the Lutheran *Augsburg Confession*, article XIX of the *Thirty-Nine Articles of the Church of England*, and the fourth book in Calvin's *Institutes* all sat in broad agreement: the Church's focus was on preaching the Word of God and administering the sacraments (baptism and communion). Clearly, such objectives reflect the Great Commission, although the importance of communion receives a focus in these statements that, while not found in the Great Commission itself, is elevated elsewhere in Scripture (Matt. 26:26-30; Luke 22:19-20; 1 Cor. 11:23-26). To make disciples, it's crucial that the Word of God is rightly taught and the sacraments rightly administered.

We're Called to Sing Praises to God.

Unfortunately, the 21st century evangelical church tends to view worship as synonymous only with singing. As we've already seen, worship is about bringing God glory in all we do. But this isn't to say that singing praises to the Lord is unimportant. Indeed, it's a vital component of our worship.

Colossians 3:16 instructs believers to "Let the word of Christ dwell richly among you, in all wisdom teaching and admonishing one another through psalms, hymns, and spiritual songs, singing to God with gratitude in your hearts." Ephesians 5:19 has a similar call, directing us to speak "to one another in psalms, hymns, and spiritual songs, singing and making music with your heart to the Lord." 1 Corinthians 14:26 elevates the importance of bringing "a hymn, a teaching, a revelation, a tongue, or an interpretation" whenever believers come together. Indeed, we have reason to believe that the Magnificat—Mary's spontaneous praise in

Guideline 7: Keep an Undistracted Focus on the Church's Mission

Luke 1 after encountering the angel Gabriel and visiting Elizabeth—was a song. Paul and Silas sing in prison (Acts 16:25). Even Jesus himself sings a hymn after the Last Supper (Matt. 26:30). Clearly, our sung praise and worship is a part of fulfilling the Church's mission.

We're Called to Pray.

Prayer isn't an afterthought. It's an *essential* imperative of the Church. In his book *Letters to the Church*, Francis Chan is characteristically direct on the matter:

> If prayer isn't vital for your church, then your church isn't vital. This statement may be bold, but I believe it's true. If you can accomplish your church's mission without daily, passionate prayer, then your mission is insufficient and your church is irrelevant.[9]

Why is Chan so strong on this? Consider the following:

- Jesus regularly prayed to his Father (Matt. 11:25-26; 26:36-46; 27:46; Mark 14:32-42; 15:34; Luke 6:12; 9:28-29; 22:32, 39-46; 23:34; 24:30-31, 50-33).
- He taught us to do the same (Matt. 5:5-6; 6:9-13 7:7-11; 21:21-22; Luke 11:2-4).
- We're called to "Rejoice always, pray constantly, give thanks in everything; for this is God's will for you in Christ Jesus" (1 Thess. 5:16-18).
- The Bible teaches us not to worry about anything,

> but in everything, through prayer and petition with thanksgiving, present our requests to God (Phil. 4:6).
> - 1 John 5:14-15 reminds us that, "This is the confidence we have before him: if we ask anything according to his will, he hears us. And if we know that he hears whatever we ask, we know that we have what we have asked of him."

Examples abound, and not just in the New Testament. In *Does Prayer Change Things?*, R. C. Sproul explores the results of prayer in the Old Testament:

> By prayer, Esau's heart was changed towards Jacob, so that they met in a friendly, rather than hostile, manner (Gen. 32).
> By the prayer of Moses, God brought the plagues upon Egpyt and then removed them again (Ex. 7-11).
> By prayer, Joshua made the sun stand still (Josh. 10).
> By prayer, when Samson was ready to perish with thirst, God brought water out of a hollow place for his sustenance (Judg. 15).
> By prayer, the strength of Samson was restored. He pulled down the temple of Dagon on the Philistines, so that those whom he killed as he died were more than all he had killed in his life (Judg. 16).
> By prayer, Elijah held back the rains for three and a half years. Then by prayer, he caused it

to rain again (1 Kings 17-18).
By the prayer of Hezekiah, God sent an angel and killed in one night 185,000 men in Sennacherib's army (2 Kings 19).
By the prayer of Asa, God confounded the army of Zerah (2 Chron. 14).[10]

Prayer has been—and will continue to be—pivotal to the lives of faithful men and women in pursuing the Church's mission.

We're Called to Provide Physical, Emotional, and Spiritual Care.

As believers, we're commanded to provide care for those around us, particularly fellow brothers and sisters in Christ. It starts with love:

> I give you a new command: Love one another. Just as I have loved you, you are also to love one another. By this everyone will know that you are my disciples, if you love one another (John 13:34-35).

Paul emphasizes the importance of mutual care for one another within the body (1 Cor. 12:25-26), which the early Church exemplified in Acts 2:42-47. We see exhortations for believers to look beyond their interests to the interests of others (Phil. 2:4), comforting them in affliction (2 Cor. 1:4), helping the weak (1 Thess. 5:14), welcoming strangers (Matt. 25:35), bearing one another's burdens (Gal. 6:2), and expressing our worship to the Lord by looking after widows and orphans in their distress (Jam. 1:27). While all believers have a responsibility to support the spiritual lives of those around them, elders particularly bear this weight (Acts 20:28; Jam. 5:14; 1 Pet. 5:1-3; 1 Tim. 3:1-7). The Scriptures are also unambiguous about helping the poor and afflicted and pursuing justice as part of the Church's mission. There are too many passages littered throughout the pages of the Bible to include them all, but here are a few that give us a general sense of the imperative:

Proverbs 29:7: "The righteous care about justice for the poor, but the wicked have no such concern."

Isaiah 58:10: "...and if you offer yourself to the hungry, and satisfy the afflicted one, then your light will shine in the darkness, and your night will be like noonday."

Matthew 25:40: "And the King will answer them, 'Truly I tell you, whatever you did for one of the least of these brothers and sisters of mine, you did for me.'"

James. 2:15-16: "If a brother or sister is without clothes and lacks daily food and one of you says to them, 'Go in peace, stay warm, and be well fed,' but you don't give them what the body needs, what good is it?"

Micah 6:8: "Mankind, he has told each of you what is good and what it is the LORD requires of you: to act justly, to love faithfulness, and to walk humbly with your God."

Guideline 7: Keep an Undistracted Focus on the Church's Mission

It's beyond the scope of the chapter to provide a complete survey of justice and poverty. However, it should be clear that supporting those in need is a biblical command. With that in mind, it's also important to stress that while serving the poor and afflicted and standing for justice are essential objectives within our mission, they are ultimately subservient to the mission itself.

The term "social justice" has garnered significant controversy in recent years, primarily because some proponents of what is an inherently and unmistakably *biblical* idea have elevated the concept beyond its rightful place in the Church's mission, giving rise to *unbiblical* frameworks like liberation theology, radical feminism, and critical race theory. On the other hand, more conservative-leaning believers are sometimes guilty of throwing the baby out with the bathwater in response to the unhealthy elevation of justice issues and consequently reject a biblical imperative as a result. There is a tension here that believers can manage when priorities are rightly aligned with God's will.

The Church is comprised of gathered believers called to fulfill Jesus' Great Commission, in the Spirit's power, and bring about the glorious worship of God the Father. A *part* of fulfilling this mission is to serve the poor, the widow, and the afflicted. A *part* of fulfilling this mission is to promote justice issues. But these are not ends in and of themselves; we pursue these things to fulfill the Great Commission and bring God the glory he deserves.

So far, we've seen that the Church is the gathering of believers united under the leadership and authority of Jesus Christ, playing a vital role in God's plans and purposes. Its mission is to fulfill Jesus' Great Commission, the Spirit's power, and bring about the glorious worship of God the Father. To pursue this mission, the Church must preach the gospel, administer the sacraments, sing praises, raise prayers to the Lord, and provide physical, emotional, and spiritual care. With these crucial foundations in place, we must now consider them in light of the shifting sands of artificial intelligence.

Staying Focused on the Mission in an AI-Driven World

In the previous chapters, we've explored some of the enormous changes likely to occur in a landscape increasingly shaped by AI. It really is, in the words of Jacob Stern, an "everything issue."[11] As we've seen, artificial intelligence is already impacting our relationships, our economies, our cultures, our approach to and understanding of knowledge, and the realities of warfare. Increasingly, we're starting to see the spiritual impact of AI as it permeates the invisible walls of the Church, and its technological formativity begins to give rise to growing idolatry and dangerous ideologies like transhumanism. We've recognized a call to be technological semi-Luddites, where we embrace the positive aspects of AI technology but aggressively reject any areas that detract from biblical truth and practice.

There is much to ponder as the Church navigates this novel territory. As the influence and impact of AI become increasingly apparent, our congregations may grow in fear, frustration, and even anger at the changes taking place. It's a natural response to large societal shifts, and one we saw at the height of the pandemic, particularly in 2020-2021.

Guideline 7: Keep an Undistracted Focus on the Church's Mission

Such a reaction could be problematic.

My primary concern with the pandemic—which could prove instructive for conversations around AI—wasn't the prolonged debates over the efficacy of vaccines and masks. Those were all important, relevant discussions that had their place. Instead, what worried me was how quickly large portions of Christ's bride on both sides of the discussion allowed these fears or frustrations to take center stage over and above the primary mission we've discussed in this chapter. As the cultural landscape shifts and adjusts to the proliferation of AI, we must keep an undistracted focus on the mission of the Church for several reasons.

First, however influential artificial intelligence becomes in our society, it won't impact the Church's role as the gathered body of believers united under the leadership and authority of Jesus Christ. As Christ's bride, body, and the dwelling place of his Spirit, it'll always play a vital role in God's plans and purposes.

Second, however prominent artificial intelligence is in our world, it will have no impact on our call to fulfill Jesus' Great Commission, in the Spirit's power, and to bring about the glorious worship of God the Father. Indeed, AI may change *how* we execute the mission, but it'll never change the core of the mission itself.

Third, however prominent artificial intelligence is in our world, it will never change the Lord's command that his Church preach the gospel, administer the sacraments, sing praises, and lift up prayers to the Lord while providing physical, emotional, and spiritual care. Again, AI may change *how* we achieve some of those objectives, but these God-given imperatives are ultimately immutable. Whatever the state of this world, these commands will never change.

In great detail, Romans 9 reminds believers that there is only one throne over all, and it belongs to the Lord of all Creations. The Lord's decree will prevail (Prov. 19:21), and he works everything out in agreement with the purpose of his will (Eph. 1:11). Because believers serve a sovereign King, there can be no truly existential threat that would thwart God's will.

If you're involved in any sort of church leadership, part of your role during these coming changes is to remind believers that Jesus will one day return (Acts 1:11; 1 Thess. 4:16-17; Rev. 1:7). What's more, he will return to an existent and waiting humanity. With every issue that causes significant anxiety (e.g., artificial intelligence, nuclear threats, climate change), believers must remember the critical and comforting truth. Jesus will not return to an empty, barren wasteland with great fanfare and suddenly realize that humans annihilated themselves before He arrived. God will not reach the consummation of his plans and utter the words, "Oops. I probably should have done this sooner."

On the other hand, there is no room for complacency. If we believe the Word of God to be infallible and true, we can certainly rejoice that the world *will not* be destroyed before Jesus returns, but that does not mean it's immune from devastating, irreparable damage and destruction. For this reason, we must act on our call to function wisely as God's stewards on the earth. Make no mistake: we are living in unprecedented times.

There is much reason to be concerned.

Guideline 7: Keep an Undistracted Focus on the Church's Mission

But there is *far greater* reason to place our trust and faith in the King eternal, immortal, invisible, the only God, who is worthy of our honor and glory forever and ever (1 Tim. 1:17).

Our mission as the Church is unchanging, and with God, it's eminently possible. Whatever awaits us in a future shaped by AI, our focus on that mission must be unchanging, too.

Reflection Questions for Guideline 7: Keep an Undistracted Focus on the Mission of the Church

1. What are some of the potential challenges that the global Church may face in staying focused on its mission in an AI-driven world?

2. What are some of the areas that distract you most from the Church's mission?

3. How can the Church's mission guide our response to artificial intelligence?

4. What personal steps can you take to ensure that you stay committed to the Church's mission?

5. How does our focus on the Church's mission help us avoid both apathy and overreactions to AI?

Guideline 7: Keep an Undistracted Focus on the Church's Mission

NOTES

[1] Wayne A Grudem, *Systematic Theology: An Introduction to Biblical Doctrine* (Grand Rapids, MI: Zondervan Academic, 2020), 1506.

[2] Mark Dever, *The Church: The Gospel Made Visible*, Digital Edition, v.1. (Nashville, TN: B&H Publishing Group, 2012), 11-12.

[3] Robert Letham, *Systematic Theology* (Wheaton, IL: Crossway, 2019), 793.

[4] Ibid.

[5] Kevin DeYoung and Greg Gilbert, *What Is the Mission of the Church?* (Wheaton, IL: Crossway, 2011), 62.

[6] John Piper, *Desiring God*, Revised Edition. (New York, NY: Multnomah Books, 2011), 18.

[7] John Piper, *Let the Nations Be Glad!: The Supremacy of God in Missions*, Third Edition. (Grand Rapids, MI: Baker Academic, 2010), Kindle Loc. 4657 of 5376.

[8] D A Carson, *Matthew (Expositor's Bible Commentary)* (Grand Rapids: Zondervan, 1984), 596.

[9] Francis Chan, *Letters to the Church* (Colorado Springs, CO: David C Cook, 2018), Kindle loc. 637 of 2302.

[10] R C Sproul, *Does Prayer Change Things?* (Lake Mary, FL: Reformation Trust Publishing, 2009), 76-77.

[11] Jacob Stern, "Where's the AI Culture War?," *The Atlantic*, last modified April 9, 2023, accessed May 19, 2023, https://www.theatlantic.com/technology/archive/2023/04/generative-ai-tech-elon-musk-chatgpt-politics-biden/673673/.

Conclusion

At the time of writing, we're almost a quarter of the way through the 21st Century, a period arguably defined by individualism, technological advances, economic and political turbulence, and a war on terror. There's little doubt that each of these areas is significant, but I propose that something else has defined this period in a subtle but powerful way: a growing addiction to the pursuit of human *omnipresence*.

For young people, the early 2000s were marked by instant messengers and texting but limited by expensive phone and internet plans. I was a member of the early teenage generation continually "present" through digital mediums. Less than a decade after the great fears of the millennium bug subsided, the iPhone arrived, altering the fabric of society. Social media burst into public consciousness in a new way with Facebook, Twitter, and Instagram. News outlets were increasingly online, instant, and adjusting content in an attempt to lure readers from an arena oversaturated with information.

Fast forward to 2024, and as we've seen, people now connect, date, consume news, and even exercise through digital mediums. In my work for an online Bible college, I regularly interact in an online space with vast swathes of people I have never met face to face. The chances are, you do, too. We're glued to those little digital portals we call cell phones more than ever. A *Reviews.org* study reports that 57% of Americans are addicted to their phones (with doubtless more in denial), and almost 90% check their phone within the first ten minutes of waking up.[1] On average, participants in the study spent roughly 4.5 hours on their phones each day. Of course, this does not include PC or laptop usage, which catapults our consumption of the digital world into considerably higher volumes.

Simply put, we're more present and connected to the world than we would have thought possible a century ago.

And that's not always a good thing.

Studies are beginning to shine a light on just how disastrous social media and the need to be continually present have been for teenagers. Research from JAMA Pediatrics in January 2023 showed that excessive social media use during adolescence can have severe consequences for a person's mental and emotional state, as well as their ability to function in the world.[2] In adults, the situation isn't much better. An article in the *American Journal of Epidemiology* showed that the use of Facebook was negatively associated with several factors, including physical health, mental health, and life satisfaction.[3] The issues go further than social media. News consumption also adds to this presence problem. At the *American Psychological Association*, Charlotte Huff notes the rise of terms like "doomscrolling," "headline anxiety," and "headline stress disorder."[4] She cites examples of studies during the pandemic that found the more people consumed COVID-related news, the worse one's mental health. However, growing studies are showing evidence that prolonged exposure to negative or "problematic news" is detrimental, eroding resilience and coping capacities.[5]

We could go on.

These are issues that affect production as well as consumption. Take so-called "multitasking," for example. In *The Organized Mind*, Daniel Levitin writes:

> Multitasking has been found to increase the production of the stress hormone cortisol as well as the fight-or-flight hormone adrenaline, which can overstimulate your brain and cause mental fog or scrambled thinking. Multitasking creates a dopamine-addiction feedback loop, effectively rewarding the brain for losing focus and for constantly searching for external stimulation.[6]

When we try to multitask, we're really trying to be present in more than one place at once. Perhaps ambipresent rather than omnipresent, but the dangers are clear. Studies show that the unhealthy desire to be present beyond our intended human capacity is quite literally wrecking our brains.

We just weren't designed that way.

Jen Wilkin spots the problem in her book *None Like Him*: "By tethering our spirits to a body, God decrees that we will be present where we are and nowhere else. Yet God, who is spirit, is able to be everywhere fully present."[7]

True Omnipresence

Only God can be *omnipresent*. He can always be near as he fills the heavens and the earth (Job. 23:23-24). He can simultaneously be seated in a static place (Psa. 33:13-14) and yet be in all places. He not only possesses the ability to see all people in all places at the same time, but he actively chooses to *observe* his creation (Job. 24:21; Prov. 15:3).

He can dwell in his people by his Spirit (1 Cor. 6:19; Rom. 8:8) and sit on his holy throne of grace (Psa. 47:8; Heb. 4:16).

Psalm 139:7-10 beautifully expresses this reality:

Where can I go to escape your Spirit?
Where can I flee from your presence?
If I go up to heaven, you are there;
if I make my bed in Sheol, you are there.
If I fly on the wings of the dawn
and settle down on the western horizon,
even there your hand will lead me;
your right hand will hold on to me.

God's omnipresence should be terrifying to those who don't know him, but for believers, this is the ultimate comfort. He is vividly present. His hand is leading us. His hand is holding onto us. This holy, merciful, grace-filled, loving God is with us.

Only God can be fully present everywhere.
We can't.
The pursuit of presence is killing us.

When we recognize that only God is present everywhere, we can be fully present where we are. We can be fully present to our friends and families, shutting ourselves off from the mixed-up notion that we need to be ambipresent to prove ourselves to the world.

We can be fully present where we are in our battle against sin. There is no space for what Jen Wilkin describes as "practical atheism"; in other words, we can't profess that God exists on a Sunday and then spend the rest of our weeks ignoring Him. Instead, we can run this race knowing that God is always with us and always helping us to become what he has already declared us to be. We can be fully present because whenever we feel lonely, abandoned, or forgotten, we know we're not. God is always with us.

What does this have to do with AI?

As we've journeyed through this book together, we've seen a rise in individualistic and perfectionist tendencies, growing relational deficits, greater division, and more confusion around exactly what constitutes "true" than ever before. Our desire to be all things to all people at all times is making us unhealthy, lonely, and miserable. All this at a time when our world faces the sort of profound economic and societal change beyond anything we've ever seen in our history. AI could change everything: our relationships, our efficiency, our ministry. Yet, socially, humans are more disconnected than ever. If we don't ensure careful guidelines, principles, and guardrails are in place, increasing the use of artificial intelligence won't make life easier for us. In fact, our relentless pursuit of human omnipresence could be the final straw that breaks the camel's back.

One of the celebrated ideals of artificial intelligence is that it will make us more "present" than ever before. As we saw in Guideline 6, transhumanists are striving to untether us from these pesky bodies. As Guideline 1 showed us, AI clones and even AI girlfriends are rising to prominence. These are just two examples of humans trying to utilize AI to become omnipresent—or at least give the illusion of it. The current effects of such a pursuit are at risk of causing irreparable damage to society. How much more damaging might the rapid development of AI become?

What do we do?

Before AI—the Great Exacerbater—pushes the issue to potentially dangerous conclusions, we must remember how to be fully present in one place at one time. It's crucial to recognize that God alone is omnipresent, and we're not. Because only God is present everywhere, we can be fully present where we are.

With this in mind, we've explored seven guidelines for ministry on the digital frontiers:

1. Prioritize Relationships.
2. Nurture Resilient Congregations.
3. Build Adaptability into Church Structures.
4. Embrace Positive Technological Developments.
5. Stay Informed in a Rapidly Changing Environment.
6. Be Proactive in Praying for God-Given Wisdom.
7. Keep an Undistracted Focus on the Mission of the Church.

It's not a comprehensive list by any means, but it's a start. By using these guidelines as guardrails during our journey into the unknown, we can be a Church that reflects the incalculable love of God to the world, builds our house on the Rock, innovates for the sake of the gospel, and pushes forward confident in the knowledge that as sons and daughters of the Lord God Almighty, we can build his Church and the gates of Hades will not overpower it (Matt. 16:18).

My prayer as you conclude this book is that you will step out in faith, not as techno-optimists or techno-pessimists, necessarily, but as the sort of biblically-minded, Jesus-centric Semi-Luddites who cautiously explore technology for the glory of the Lord, rejecting anything that diverts us from the great call of his mission.

If we're careful, we just might find a world of gospel opportunity where the Church and AI meet.

What an exciting thought!

May God give us the courage and wisdom to seize it.

NOTES

¹ Alex Kerai, "Cell Phone Usage Statistics: Mornings Are for Notifications," *Reviews.Org*, last modified July 21, 2023, accessed February 15, 2024, https://www.reviews.org/mobile/cell-phone-addiction/.

² Maria T. Maza et al., "Association of Habitual Checking Behaviors on Social Media With Longitudinal Functional Brain Development," *JAMA Pediatrics* 177, no. 2 (February 1, 2023): 160–167.

³ H. B. Shakya and N. A. Christakis, "Association of Facebook Use With Compromised Well-Being: A Longitudinal Study," *American journal of epidemiology* 185, no. 3 (2017): 203–211.

⁴ Charlotte Huff, "Media Overload Is Hurting Our Mental Health. Here Are Ways to Manage Headline Stress," *Https://Www.Apa.Org*, last modified 2022, accessed February 15, 2024, https://www.apa.org/monitor/2022/11/strain-media-overload.

⁵ Natascha de Hoog and Peter Verboon, "Is the News Making Us Unhappy? The Influence of Daily News Exposure on Emotional States," *British Journal of Psychology* 111, no. 2 (2019): 157–173; Bryan McLaughlin, Melissa R. Gotlieb, and Devin J. Mills, "Caught in a Dangerous World: Problematic News Consumption and Its Relationship to Mental and Physical Ill-Being," *Health Communication* 38, no. 12 (October 15, 2023): 2687–2697.

⁶ Daniel J. Levitin, *The Organized Mind* (Toronto: Allen Lane, 2014), Kindle Loc. 1985 of 11437.

⁷ Jen Wilkin, *None Like Him* (Wheaton, IL.: Crossway, 2016), Kindle Loc. 1189 of 2240.

Bibliography

Achenbach, Joel, and Laurie McGinley. "Another Casualty of the Coronavirus Pandemic: Trust in Government Science." *The Washington Post*. Last modified 2020. Accessed September 6, 2021. https://www.washingtonpost.com/health/covid-trust-in-science/2020/10/11/b6048c14-03e1-11eb-a2db-417cddf4816a_story.html.

Adams. "Artificial Intelligence: 'We're like Children Playing with a Bomb' | Artificial Intelligence (AI) | The Guardian." Last modified June 12, 2016. Accessed May 22, 2023. https://www.theguardian.com/technology/2016/jun/12/nick-bostrom-artificial-intelligence-machine.

Addley, Esther. "'AI' Named Most Notable Word of 2023 by Collins Dictionary." *The Guardian*, November 1, 2023, sec. Technology. Accessed December 17, 2023. https://www.theguardian.com/technology/2023/nov/01/ai-named-most-notable-word-of-2023-by-collins-dictionary.

Andersen, Ross. "Never Give Artificial Intelligence the Nuclear Codes." *The Atlantic*. Last modified May 2, 2023. Accessed May 19, 2023. https://www.theatlantic.com/magazine/archive/2023/06/ai-warfare-nuclear-weapons-strike/673780/.

Aquinas, Thomas. *Summa Theologica*, n.d.

Armstrong, Martin. "Friendships: Less Is Now More." *World Economic Forum*. Last modified November 3, 2022. Accessed February 2, 2024. https://www.weforum.org/agenda/2022/11/friendships-less-is-now-more/.

Asimov, Isaac. *Book of Science and Nature Quotations*. Edited by Isaac Asimov and Jason A. Schulman. New York, NY: Weidenfeld & Nicolson, 1988.

Barton, Bruce B, P. W. Comfort, G. Osborne, L. K. Taylor, and D. Verrman. *Life Application New Testament Commentary*. Wheaton, Ill.: Tyndale House Publishers, 2001.

Bedard, Alex. "The 8-Step Process for Leading Change | Dr. John Kotter." *Kotter International Inc*, n.d. Accessed February 10, 2024. https://www.kotterinc.com/methodology/8-steps/.

Bostrom, Nick. *Superintelligence*. Oxford: Oxford University Press, 2014.

Brumfiel, Geoff. "Artificial Intelligence Can Find Your Location in Photos, Worrying Privacy Experts." *NPR*, December 19, 2023, sec. Technology. Accessed December 20, 2023. https://www.npr.org/2023/12/19/1219984002/artificial-intelligence-can-find-your-location-in-photos-worrying-privacy-expert.

Carroll, Lewis. *Alice's Adventures in Wonderland*. Seattle: Amazon Classics, 1866.

Carson, D A. *Matthew (Expositor's Bible Commentary)*. Grand Rapids: Zondervan, 1984.

Cawthorne, Nigel. *Alan Turing: The Enigma Man*. E Book. Arcturus Publishings Limited, 2014.

Chace, Calum. *Surviving AI*. Third Edition. Three Cs, 2020.

Chan, Francis. *Letters to the Church*. Colorado Springs, CO: David C Cook, 2018.

Corpuz, Jeff Clyde G. "Adapting to the Culture of 'New Normal': An Emerging Response to COVID-19." *Journal of Public Health* 43, no. 2 (June 7, 2021): e344–e345.

Crawford, Robyn. "High Internet Use Leads to Low Self-Esteem: Study." *Global News*. Last modified 2017. Accessed February 3, 2024. https://globalnews.ca/news/3261027/high-internet-use-leads-to-low-self-esteem-study/.

Daugherty, Paul. "A.I. Will Potentially Impact 40% of Your Working Hours, According to Accenture." *Fortune*. Last modified 2023. Accessed July 21, 2023. https://fortune.com/2023/05/11/ai-impact-work-hours-accenture-careers-tech-paul-daugherty/.

Davenport, Thomas H., and Rajeev Ronanki. "Artificial Intelligence for the Real World." In *HBR's 10 Must Reads On AI, Analytics, and the New Machine Age*. Boston, MA: Harvard Business Review Press, 2019.

Dever, Mark. *The Church: The Gospel Made Visible*. Digital Edition, v.1. Nashville, TN: B&H Publishing Group, 2012.

DeYoung, Kevin, and Greg Gilbert. *What Is the Mission of the Church?* Wheaton, IL: Crossway, 2011.

Dickinson, Kevin. "New AI Translates 5,000-Year-Old Cuneiform Tablets Instantly." *Big Think*, July 4, 2023. Accessed December 8, 2023. https://bigthink.com/the-future/ai-translates-cuneiform/.

Doucleff, Michaeleen. "The Truth about Teens, Social Media and the Mental Health Crisis." *NPR*. Last modified April 25, 2023. Accessed February 3, 2024. https://www.npr.org/sections/health-shots/2023/04/25/1171773181/social-media-teens-mental-health.

Drug, Fight the New. "10 Negative Effects of Porn on Your Brain, Body, Relationships, and Society." *Fight the New Drug*, n.d. Accessed February 2, 2024. https://fightthenewdrug.org/10-reasons-why-porn-is-unhealthy-for-consumers-and-society/.

Edwards, Benj. "Deepfake Scammer Walks off with $25 Million in First-of-Its-Kind AI Heist." *Ars Technica*. Last modified February 5, 2024. Accessed February 14, 2024. https://arstechnica.com/information-technology/2024/02/deepfake-scammer-walks-off-with-25-million-in-first-of-its-kind-ai-heist/.

Emery White, James. *Meet Generation Z: Understanding and Reaching the New Post-Christian World*. Ebook Edition. Grand Rapids, MI: Baker Books, 2017.

Europol Innovations Lab. *Facing Reality? Law Enforcement and the Challenge of Deepfakes*. Luxembourg: Publications Office of the European Union, 2022.

Evans, Stephen C. "Relativism." In *Pocket Dictionary of Apologetics & Philosophy of Religion*. Downers Grove, IL: Inter-Varsity Press, 2002.

———. "Subjectivism." In *Pocket Dictionary of Apologetics & Philosophy of Religion*. Downer's Grove, IL: Inter-Varsity Press, 2002.

Fetters, Ashley. "The Five Years That Changed Dating." *The Atlantic*, December 21, 2018. Accessed February 1, 2024. https://www.theatlantic.com/family/archive/2018/12/tinder-changed-dating/578698/.

Foxe, John. "The Invention and Benefit of Printing (c. 1563)." In *The Acts and Monuments of John Foxe*, edited by Stephen Reed Cattley, 3:718–22. London: R. B. Seeley and W. Burnside, 1837.

Frederick, John, and Eric Lewellen, eds. *The HTML of Cruciform Love: Towards a Theology of the Internet*. Eugene, OR: Pickwick Publications, 2019.

Frey, Carl Benedikt, and Michael A. Osborne. "The Future of Employment: How Susceptible Are Jobs to Computerisation?" *Technological Forecasting and Social Change* 114 (2017): 254–280.

Garcia, Justin R. "Sexual Hookup Culture: A Review." *Review of General Psychology* 16, no. 2 (2012).

González, Justo L. *The Story of Christianity Volume One: The Early Church to the Reformation*. New York, NY: HarperCollins Publishers Inc., 2010.

Good, I. J. "Speculations Concerning the First UItraintelligent Machine." *Advanced in Computers* 6 (1966): 31–88.

Green, Justin. "Experts Warn of Rise in Scammers Using AI to Mimic Voices of Loved Ones in Distress." *ABC News*. Last modified July 7, 2023. Accessed December 19, 2023. https://abcnews.go.com/Technology/experts-warn-rise-scammers-ai-mimic-voices-loved/story?id=100769857.

Grudem, Wayne A. *Systematic Theology: An Introduction to Biblical Doctrine*. Grand Rapids, MI: Zondervan Academic, 2020.

Haidt, Jonathan. *The Righteous Mind*. New York, NY: Pantheon Books, 2012.

Hambling, David. "Israel Rolls Out Legion-X Drone Swarm For The Urban Battlefield." *Forbes*. Last modified October 24, 2022. Accessed June 2, 2023. https://www.forbes.com/sites/davidhambling/2022/10/24/israel-rolls-out-legion-x-drone-swarm-for-the-urban-battlefield/.

———. "Israel Used World's First AI-Guided Combat Drone Swarm in Gaza Attacks." *New Scientist*. Last modified June 30, 2021. Accessed June 2, 2023. https://www.newscientist.com/article/2282656-israel-used-worlds-first-ai-guided-combat-drone-swarm-in-gaza-attacks/.

Hari, Johann. *Lost Connections: Uncovering the Real Causes of Depression - and the Unexpected Solutions*. New York, NY: Bloomsbury Publishing, 2018.

Harris, Shanice. "Have Young Adults Mentally Recovered from COVID-19?" *Northwestern*. Last modified November 23, 2023. Accessed February 5, 2024. https://news.northwestern.edu/stories/2023/11/young-adults-show-more-mental-health-distress-during-the-covid-19-pandemic-than-older-adults-study-finds/.

Hemingway, Ernest. *The Sun Also Rises*. E-Book. New York, NY: Scribner, 2014.

Hern, Alex. "Stephen Hawking: AI Will Be 'either Best or Worst Thing' for Humanity." *The Guardian*, October 19, 2016, sec. Science. Accessed July 21, 2023. https://www.theguardian.com/science/2016/oct/19/stephen-hawking-ai-best-or-worst-thing-for-humanity-cambridge.

Hirsch, Rudolf. *Printing, Selling and Reading, 1450-1550*. Wiesbaden: Otto Harrassowitz, 1974.

de Hoog, Natascha, and Peter Verboon. "Is the News Making Us Unhappy? The Influence of Daily News Exposure on Emotional States." *British Journal of Psychology* 111, no. 2 (2019): 157–173.

Houser, Kristen. "Meta's First-of-Its-Kind AI Can Translate between Any of 100 Languages." *Freethink*, August 31, 2023. Accessed December 8, 2023. https://www.freethink.com/robots-ai/universal-translator.

Huff, Charlotte. "Media Overload Is Hurting Our Mental Health. Here Are Ways to Manage Headline Stress." *Https://Www.Apa.Org*. Last modified 2022. Accessed February 15, 2024. https://www.apa.org/monitor/2022/11/strain-media-overload.

Hutson, Matthew. "Artificial Intelligence Goes Bilingual—without a Dictionary." Last modified 2017. Accessed July 26, 2023. https://www.science.org/content/article/artificial-intelligence-goes-bilingual-without-dictionary.

Huxley, Julian. "Transhumanism." *Journal of Humanistic Psychology* 8, no. 1 (1957): 73–76.

Iansiti, Marco, and Karim R. Lakhani. "Managing Our Hub Economy." In *HBR's 10 Must Reads On AI, Analytics, and the New Machine Age*. Boston, MA: Harvard Business Review Press, 2019.

Jones, Jeffrey M. "US Church Membership Falls Below Majority for First Time." *Gallup.Com*. Last modified March 29, 2021. Accessed February 5, 2024. https://news.gallup.com/poll/341963/church-membership-falls-below-majority-first-time.aspx.

Keller, Timothy. *Center Church*. Grand Rapids, MI: Zondervan, 2012.

à Kempis, Thomas. *The Imitation of Christ*. Translated by William Benham, 1886.

Kerai, Alex. "Cell Phone Usage Statistics: Mornings Are for Notifications." *Reviews.Org*. Last modified July 21, 2023. Accessed February 15, 2024. https://www.reviews.org/mobile/cell-phone-addiction/.

Keynes, John Maynard. "Economic Possibilities for Our Grandchildren." In *Essays in Persuasion*, 358–373. New York: W. W. Norton & Co., 1960.

Koizumi, Kenkichiro. "Technology at a Crossroads: The Fifth Generation Computer Project in Japan." *Historical Studies in the Physical and Biological Sciences* 37, no. 2 (2007): 355–368.

Komando, Kim. "Love Is in the A.I.r: NYC Mom, 36, Marries Virtual Husband 'Eren.'" *Mail Online*. Last modified June 3, 2023. Accessed January 27, 2024. https://www.dailymail.co.uk/sciencetech/article-12153131/Love-r-Bronx-mom-36-marries-virtual-husband-Eren.html.

Korosec, Kirsten. "Anthony Levandowski Closes His Church of AI." *TechCrunch*, February 18, 2021. Accessed May 22, 2023. https://techcrunch.com/2021/02/18/anthony-levandowski-closes-his-church-of-ai/.

Kramer, Stephanie. "US Has World's Highest Rate of Children Living in Single-Parent Households." *Pew Research Center*, n.d. Accessed February 1, 2024. https://www.pewresearch.org/short-reads/2019/12/12/u-s-children-more-likely-than-children-in-other-countries-to-live-with-just-one-parent/.

Kreeft, Peter. *C. S. Lewis for the Third Millenium: Six Essays on the Abolition of Man*. San Francisco, CA: Ignatius Press, 1994.

Kumar, Vinayak, and Ram Prasad Modalavalasa. "5 Lasting Changes from the COVID-19 Pandemic." *ABC News*. Last modified 2020. Accessed September 6, 2021. https://abcnews.go.com/Health/lasting-covid-19-pandemic/story?id=72393992.

Lai, Richard. "Samsung Teases Its Own AI-Based Real-Time Phone Call Translation." *Engadget*. Last modified November 9, 2023. Accessed December 8, 2023. https://www.engadget.com/samsung-teases-its-own-ai-based-real-time-phone-call-translation-053818106.html.

Lee, Kai-Fu, and Chen Qiufan. *AI 2041*. New York: Currency, 2021.

Leithart, Peter J. *Defending Constantine: The Twilight of an Empire and the Dawn of Christendom*. Downer's Grove, IL: IVP Academic, 2010.

Lennox, John C. *2084: Artificial Intelligence and the Future of Humanity*. Grand Rapids, MI: Zondervan Reflective, 2020.

Letham, Robert. *Systematic Theology*. Wheaton, IL: Crossway, 2019.

Lewis, C S. "The Abolition of Man." In *The Complete C. S. Lewis*. Toronto: McClelland & Stewart, 2014.

———. "The Poison of Subjectivism." In *Christian Reflections*, edited by Walter Hooper. Grand Rapids, MI: William B. Eerdmans Publishing Company, 1967.

Llach, Laura. "Meet the First Spanish AI Model Who Earns up to €10,000 per Month." *Euronews*. Last modified January 20, 2024. Accessed February 6, 2024. https://www.euronews.com/next/2024/01/20/meet-the-first-spanish-ai-model-earning-up-to-10000-per-month.

Lorenz, Taylor. "An Influencer's AI Clone Will Be Your Girlfriend for $1 a Minute." *Washington Post*. Washington, DC., May 13, 2023. Accessed July 24, 2023. https://www.washingtonpost.com/technology/2023/05/13/caryn-ai-technology-gpt-4/.

Lowrey, Annie. "Before AI Takes Over, Make Plans to Give Everyone Money." *The Atlantic*. Last modified May 17, 2023. Accessed May 19, 2023. https://www.theatlantic.com/ideas/archive/2023/05/ai-job-losses-policy-support-universal-basic-income/674071/.

Markos, Louis. *From Plato to Christ: How Platonic Thought Shaped the Christian Faith*. Downer's Grove, IL: IVP Academic, 2021.

Matzko, Paul. "Meet the Pioneering Radio Preachers Who Revolutionized Religious Broadcasting." *ChristianityToday.Com*. Last modified June 28, 2022. Accessed December 7, 2023. https://www.christianitytoday.com/ct/2022/june-web-only/ministers-new-medium-fulton-sheen-walter-maier-radio.html.

Mayor, Adrienne. *Gods and Robots*. Princeton, NJ: Princeton University Press, 2018.

Maza, Maria T., Kara A. Fox, Seh-Joo Kwon, Jessica E. Flannery, Kristen A. Lindquist, Mitchell J. Prinstein, and Eva H. Telzer. "Association of Habitual Checking Behaviors on Social Media With Longitudinal Functional Brain Development." *JAMA Pediatrics* 177, no. 2 (February 1, 2023): 160–167.

McCarthy, J., M. L. Minsky, N. Rochester, and C. E. Shannon. "A Proposal for the Dartmouth Summer Research Project on Artificial Intelligence, August 31, 1955." Ai Magazine 27, no. 4 (2006).

McCracken, Brett. *The Wisdom Pyramid*. Wheaton, IL.: Crossway, 2021.

McLaughlin, Bryan, Melissa R. Gotlieb, and Devin J. Mills. "Caught in a Dangerous World: Problematic News Consumption and Its Relationship to Mental and Physical Ill-Being." *Health Communication* 38, no. 12 (October 15, 2023): 2687–2697.

Merchant, Brian. *Blood in the Machine*. New York: Little, Brown and Company, 2023.

Metz, Cade. *Genius Makers*. New York, NY: Dutton, 2021.

Milmo, Dan, and Alex Hern. "Google Chief Admits 'Biased' AI Tool's Photo Diversity Offended Users." The Guardian, February 28, 2024, sec. Technology. Accessed March 16, 2024. https://www.theguardian.com/technology/2024/feb/28/google-chief-ai-tools-photo-diversity-offended-users.

Mur Effing, Mercé. "The Origin and Development of Self-Help Literature in the United States: The Concept of Success and Happiness, an Overview." Journal of the Spanish Association of Anglo-American Studies 31, no. 2 (2009): 125–141.

Neve, Jan-Emmanuel De, and George Ward. "Does Work Make You Happy? Evidence from the World Happiness Report." *Harvard Business Review*, March 20, 2017. Accessed May 22, 2023. https://hbr.org/2017/03/does-work-make-you-happy-evidence-from-the-world-happiness-report.

Newport, Frank. "The Impact of Shifts in American Culture." *Gallup*. Last modified 2021. Accessed September 7, 2021. https://news.gallup.com/opinion/polling-matters/353216/impact-shifts-american-culture.aspx.

O'Gieblyn, Meghan. *God, Human, Animal, Machine*. New York, NY: Doubleday, 2021.

Perry, Louise. *The Case Against the Sexual Revolution*. Cambridge: Polity Press, 2022.

Peterson, Eugene H. *The Contemplative Pastor*. Grand Rapids, MI: William B. Eerdmans Publishing Company, 1989.

Piper, John. *Desiring God*. Revised Edition. New York, NY: Multnomah Books, 2011.

Piper, John. *Let the Nations Be Glad!: The Supremacy of God in Missions*. Third Edition. Grand Rapids, MI: Baker Academic, 2010.

Plato. "Theaetus," n.d.

Porter, Michael E., and James E. Heppelmann. "Why Every Organization Needs an Augmented Reality Strategy." In *HBR's 10 Must Reads On AI, Analytics, and the New Machine Age*. Boston, MA: Harvard Business Review Press, 2019.

Rae, Scott B. *Moral Choices: An Introduction to Ethics*. Grand Rapids, MI: Zondervan, 2009.

Rainer, Thom. S. *The Post-Quarantine Church: Six Urgent Challenges and Opportunities That Will Determine the Future of Your Congregation*. Carol Stream, IL.: Tyndale, 2020.

Rawat. "Transhumanism: Savior of Humanity or False Prophecy?" *Big Think*, July 27, 2022. Accessed May 5, 2023. https://bigthink.com/the-future/transhumanism-savior-humanity-false-prophecy/.

Rodriguez Martinez, Marta, Tom Goodwin, and Naira Davlashyan. "What the Ex-Tinder Boss Thinks about the Future of Dating." *Euronews*. Last modified November 22, 2023. Accessed February 1, 2024. https://www.euronews.com/business/2023/11/22/loneliness-is-biggest-threat-after-climate-crisis-ex-tinder-boss-says-ai-will-fix-relation.

Rogers, Mark. "Christian History: Broadcasting the Gospel." *Christianity Today*. Last modified 2010. Accessed December 7, 2023. https://www.christianitytoday.com/history/2010/march/broadcasting-gospel.html.

Rosenberg, Louis. "Huge Milestone as Human Subject Wears Augmented Reality Contact Lens for First Time." *Big Think*, July 6, 2022. Accessed December 8, 2023. https://bigthink.com/the-future/augmented-reality-ar-milestone-wearable-contacts/.

Rosiak, Luke. "School Board Member Sworn In On Stack Of Gay Porn Instead Of Bible." *The Daily Wire*. Last modified December 14, 2023. Accessed February 5, 2024. https://www.dailywire.com/news/school-board-member-sworn-in-on-stack-of-gay-porn-instead-of-bible.

Rosner, Elizabeth. "US Divorce Rates Skyrocket amid COVID-19 Pandemic." *New York Post*. Last modified 2020. Accessed September 6, 2021. https://nypost.com/2020/09/01/divorce-rates-skyrocket-in-u-s-amid-covid-19/.

Russell, Stuart. *Human Compatible: Artificial Intelligence and the Problem of Control*. New York, NY: Penguin Books, 2019.

Santos, Henri C., Michael E. W. Varnum, and Igor Grossmann. "Global Increases in Individualism." *Psychological Science* 28, no. 9 (2017): 1228–1239.

Schaff, P. "Article IV: Constantine the Great, and the Downfall of Paganism in the Roman Empire." *Bibliotecha Sacra* 20, no. 80 (1863).

Schmidt, Jonathan Haidt, Eric. "AI Is About to Make Social Media (Much) More Toxic." *The Atlantic*. Last modified May 5, 2023. Accessed July 21, 2023. https://www.theatlantic.com/technology/archive/2023/05/generative-ai-social-media-integration-dangers-disinformation-addiction/673940/.

Schubarth, Cromwell. "Bay Area Startup Mojo Vision Puts Smart Contact Lenses on Hold, Cuts Staff by 75%." *Silicon Valley Business Journal*. Last modified January 6, 2023. Accessed December 8, 2023. https://www.bizjournals.com/sanjose/news/2023/01/06/saratoga-based-mojo-vision-cuts-staff-by-75.html.

Schuurman, Derek C. "Artificial Intelligence: Discerning a Christian Response." *Perspectives on Science and Christian Faith* 71, no. 2 (2019).

Shakya, H. B., and N. A. Christakis. "Association of Facebook Use With Compromised Well-Being: A Longitudinal Study." *American journal of epidemiology* 185, no. 3 (2017): 203–211.

Sheetz, Kyle H., Jake Claflin, and Justin B. Dimick. "Trends in the Adoption of Robotic Surgery for Common Surgical Procedures." *JAMA Network Open* 3, no. 1 (January 10, 2020): e1918911–e1918911.

Shelley, Bruce. *Church History in Plain Language*. Grand Rapids: HarperCollins Christian Publishing, 2013.

Shweder, R. A., N. C. Much, M. Mahapatra, and L. Park. "The 'Big Three' of Morality (Autonomy, Community, Divinity) and the 'Big Three' Explanations of Suffering." *Morality and Health* (1997): 119–169.

Smith, Christian, ed. "Introduction: Rethinking the Secularization of American Public Life." In *The Secular Revolution: Power, Interests, and Conflict in the Secularization of American Public Life*. Los Angeles, CA: University of California Press, 2003.

Smith, Zachary G. "Gnosticism." In *The Lexham Bible Dictionary*, 2016.

Sproul, R. C. *Does Prayer Change Things?* Lake Mary, FL: Reformation Trust Publishing, 2009.

Stanford University. "Ancient Myths Reveal Early Fantasies about Artificial Life." *Stanford News*, February 28, 2019. Accessed May 22, 2023. https://news.stanford.edu/2019/02/28/ancient-myths-reveal-early-fantasies-artificial-life/.

Stern, Jacob. "Where's the AI Culture War?" *The Atlantic*. Last modified April 9, 2023. Accessed May 19, 2023. https://www.theatlantic.com/technology/archive/2023/04/generative-ai-tech-elon-musk-chatgpt-politics-biden/673673/.

Steward Holland, Sarah, and Beth Silvers. *I Think You're Wrong (But I'm Listening): A Guide to Grace-Filled Political Conversations*. Nashville, TN: Nelson Books, 2019.

Storr, Will. *Selfie: How the West Became Self-Obsessed*. London: Picador, 2018.

Talev, Margaret. "Axios-Ipsos Poll: Distrusting Big Pharma and the FDA - Axios." *Axios*. Last modified September 14, 2020. Accessed September 7, 2021. https://www.axios.com/axios-ipsos-poll-distrusting-pharma-fda-coronavirus-index-7605a67b-606d-4e0a-b85f-1887147aa8f8.html.

Taylor, Charles. *A Secular Age*. Cambridge, MA: Harvard University Press, 2007.

Thornton, A, and D Freedman. "Changing Attitudes toward Marriage and Single Life." *Fam Plann Perspect* 14, no. 6 (1982): 297–303.

Turing, A. M. "Computing Machinery and Intelligence." *Mind*, New Series 59, no. 236 (1950): 433–460.

———. "On Computable Numbers, with an Application to the Entscheidungsproblem." *Proceedings of the London Mathematical Society* 2, no. 42 (1936): 230–265.

Twenge, Jean M. "Have Smartphones Destroyed a Generation?" *The Atlantic*. Last modified August 3, 2017. Accessed July 21, 2023. https://www.theatlantic.com/magazine/archive/2017/09/has-the-smartphone-destroyed-a-generation/534198/.

Vanian, Jonathan. "Mark Zuckerberg Indicates Meta Is Spending Billions of Dollars on Nvidia AI Chips." *CNBC*. Last modified January 18, 2024. Accessed February 14, 2024. https://www.cnbc.com/2024/01/18/mark-zuckerberg-indicates-meta-is-spending-billions-on-nvidia-ai-chips.html.

Wheeler, Tom. "With New Technology Challenges, Remember We've Been Here before." *Brookings*. Last modified 2019. Accessed December 7, 2023. https://www.brookings.edu/articles/with-new-technology-challenges-remember-weve-been-here-before/.

Zahl, David. *Seculosity: How Career, Parenting, Technology, Food, Politics, and Romance Became Our New Religion and What to Do about It*. Kindle Edition. Minneapolis, MN: Fortress Press, 2019.

"2023 Global Scripture Access." *Wycliffe Global Alliance*, 2023. Accessed December 7, 2023. https://www.wycliffe.net/resources/statistics/.

"Alan Mathison Turing (1912-54)." *King's College Cambridge*. Accessed August 7, 2023. https://www.kings.cam.ac.uk/archive-centre/online-resources/online-exhibitions/alan-mathison-turing-1912-54.

"Google.Com Traffic Analytics, Ranking Stats & Tech Stack." *Similarweb*. Accessed January 6, 2024. https://www.similarweb.com/website/google.com/.

"Hookup Culture Statistics - New Survey Data On One Night Stands, Casual Sex and Hooking Up." *Bedbible Research Center*. Last modified March 17, 2023. Accessed January 31, 2024. https://bedbible.com/hookup-culture-statistics/.

"NCHS Pressroom - 1995 Fact Sheet - Advance Report of Final Divorce Statistics." Accessed February 1, 2024. https://www.cdc.gov/nchs/pressroom/95facts/fs_439s.htm.

"Opinion on the Possibility of Civil War US 2022." *Statista*. Accessed February 4, 2024. https://www.statista.com/statistics/1326688/public-opinion-possibility-civil-war/.

"Pause Giant AI Experiments: An Open Letter." *Future of Life Institute*, March 22, 2023. Accessed June 2, 2023. https://futureoflife.org/open-letter/pause-giant-ai-experiments/.

"Printing Press." *HISTORY*. Last modified June 29, 2023. Accessed August 16, 2023. https://www.history.com/topics/inventions/printing-press.

"Religious Landscape Study: Frequency of Reading Scripture." *Pew Research Center*. Accessed February 13, 2024. https://www.pewresearch.org/religion/religious-landscape-study/.

Sam Altman: OpenAI CEO on GPT-4, ChatGPT, and the Future of AI | Lex Fridman Podcast #367, 2023. Accessed January 7, 2024. https://www.youtube.com/watch?v=L_Guz73e6fw.

"Society Began Shifting towards Individualism More than a Century Ago." *Waterloo News*. Last modified February 5, 2015. Accessed February 2, 2024. https://uwaterloo.ca/news/news/society-began-shifting-towards-individualism-more-century.

"Some Pros and Cons: Shedding Light on Overhead Projection." *Reformed Worship*. Last modified 1999. Accessed December 7, 2023. https://www.reformedworship.org/article/march-1999/some-pros-and-cons-shedding-light-overhead-projection.

"Statement on AI Risk | CAIS." Accessed June 2, 2023. https://www.safe.ai/statement-on-ai-risk#sign.

"The Sophists." *Stanford Encyclopedia of Philosophy*. Last modified September 30, 2011. Accessed June 25, 2022. https://plato.stanford.edu/entries/sophists/.

"'We Love Each Other': Woman Creates and 'marries' AI Chatbot Boyfriend." *Euronews*. Last modified June 8, 2023. Accessed July 24, 2023. https://www.euronews.com/next/2023/06/07/love-in-the-time-of-ai-woman-claims-she-married-a-chatbot-and-is-expecting-its-baby.

"What Is Technological Singularity?: AI Terms Explained - AI For Anyone." Accessed May 5, 2023. https://www.aiforanyone.org/glossary/technological-singularity.

"Wisdom." *Psychology Today*. Accessed April 19, 2023. https://www.psychologytoday.com/us/basics/wisdom.

www.ingramcontent.com/pod-product-compliance
Lightning Source LLC
Chambersburg PA
CBHW030432010526
44118CB00011B/610